THE INNER CITY CARIBBEAN COOKBOOK
RECIPES COLLECTED FROM MY PAST

FIRST EDITION

This book is dedicated to my late Grandfather

And my late Mother

The Inner City Caribbean Cookbook
Recipes collected from my Past

Andrew Lloyd Brown

Photographs by T.P. Morley

Unnatural Talents Ltd

Unnatural Talents Publication Ltd

Published by 'Unnatural Talents Publication Ltd'
Unnatural Talents Publication Ltd
75, Grassington Road,
Aspley Lane
Nottingham
NG8 3PA

Unnatural Talents Publication Ltd. Registered Offices:
75, Grassington Road,
Aspley Lane
Nottingham
NG8 3PA

www.unnaturaltalents.com

First Published 2005
1

Set in
Colour Reproduction by
Printed in the Midlands, Great Britain

ISBN
0-9549504-0-2

C O N T E N T S

Introduction

What does the thought of the Caribbean conjure up in your mind? Exotic fruits like the Guavas, Papayas, Bananas and Coconuts, or is it the Vegetables from the Yam family, the Cho Cho and sweet potatoes. Perhaps it's the Rum 100% proof, neat or mixed in some wicked cocktail that will just blow your head off. All this coupled with the unrelenting heat of the tropics, watching the warm Caribbean Sea, drift in and out, with tales of piracy and battles on the high seas.

It is a magical place, where the gift from land and sea is locked in the food. Your sense is assaulted with the aromas and colours all imprint in your mind.

The Inner City Caribbean Cookbook is a combination of my traditional and modern Caribbean cooking influences. Refining dishes used over three generations.

This book represents a part of my inner city life.

The inner city cook's story

I was born and brought up in the Inner city area of Nottingham. My grandfather, Henry Gayle Johnson was a great cook who appreciated good food. With his family in Jamaica he owned a number of businesses dating back to the 1800s, including a small farm rearing livestock, land development selling all farm produce plantain, callaloo, mangos, yams, aubergine, soursop, coconuts, peanuts, gungo peas, and breadfruit at the local market, and also a store which had a bakery, grocery and butchers shop. All this was in Old Harbour in the Parish of St Catherine. He owned another Property in Old Harbour Bay from where he hunted wild boar and went shooting for a variety of birds. But he never went fishing. His mother banned him from this because his father had been shipwrecked in the Caribbean Sea, and did not return for over a year.

So my grandparents, Henry and Lena Johnson travelled to England in 1955, arriving at Southampton after 14 days at sea with an address in Robin Hood Chase, St. Ann's, Nottingham. They had had thirteen children. In 1962 my mother arrived in England. She had four children: Tony followed by Marcia and then Debrah and finally myself, Andrew, the youngest, born in 1969. My partner Tracey and I, have three children, Alannah, Tyra and Tobiyas.

I now realise how much the influence of my grandfather steered me in this direction. Memories of him making wedding cake, Jamaican bun, hard dough bread, curried goat, cow foot, ginger beer, sweet syrups and creamed ice, are still vivid in my mind. He also never possessed a set of scales but the quality of his cooking was consistent. I look back and think how amazing his constant accuracy was.

Every Thursday we would walk to the West Indian food shop on Ilkeston Road where my grandfather had shopped long before I was born, to buy a whole stack of ingredients from root ginger and seasonings to yam, plantain, breadfruit, cho-cho, mangos, green banana and scotch bonnet. I still use this shop now.

Unfortunately, grandfather died when I was 10 years old, so there were no personal records of his recipes. So for a while I have been working to make up a recipe book based mainly on memories of 20 years ago with a modern feel.

Growing up as a child my mother cooked all natural foods, nothing processed. Every Saturday we would eat a well prepared soup with cho-cho, yam, pumpkin, coco and a variety of meats such as Chicken, Mutton and Beef along with a cornmeal dumplin. This in England would be classed as a stew. She enjoyed cooking belly pork, curried mutton and braised chicken. I enjoyed the oxtail with butterbeans the most. The chicken dumplings, well, the fried dough would just melt in your mouth. She cooked the best rice I've tasted. She was domestically, Queen of Consistency. While I was a child she did not really make many desserts but she would make bread pudding and coconut drops.

It seems like the last generation are only eating Caribbean food at the few take-away's located in the inner cities, or when they visit their parents or grand parents. I too have been very much guilty of this myself. So it's time to make it more accessible to all those visitors to the Caribbean who would like to try some of the dishes and flavours they had on holiday but with a modern British twist, making everything possible to create and enjoy. I have collected and listed over a 100 recipes based on a mixture of my cooking career and the pre-training unknowingly given to me by my grandfather.

I was mis-educated throughout my schooling life. I felt this most at secondary school. Most of the subjects I was roped into at school did not in anyway gear me up for working or living life. At 10 years old I was placed in a pigeon hole and left there. I was 17 or 18 years old when I realised the schooling system had set me up to fail and to limit the way I thought and behaved. But then I was fortunate! One day at school the teacher did not turn up for my lesson so I had to join in a Home Economic group. We were making Pizza. I enjoyed this and my enjoyment was topped off when I received a 9 ½ out of 10 for my efforts. At that point, aged 13, I knew cooking was going to be the life for me.

My first real cooking post was in a Piano bar on Parliament Street. It was through a Youth Training Scheme. I went on the scheme to raise a little cash until college started, although I didn't tell them this when they accepted me. I was refused entry into the local Clarendon Catering FE College, (I had been told by my form teacher and many others I crossed on my journey of life that I would not achieve this, I would not get to West Nottinghamshire

FE College as this journey would be a daily travel of 20 miles each way by bus to Mansfield and I was nearly always late for school anyway). He was wrong!

As soon as I started College I got myself a job at the Victoria Stakis Hotel, Milton Street as a Banqueting waiter. I wasn't all that good at it but it gave me experience and allowed me to buy the things I wanted and needed. In my second year at catering college I moved to The Royal Hotel, Wollaton Street. I was taken on as an on call member of staff. I got to work everywhere, in the Carvery Kitchen, Production Kitchen, Brasserie and The French Restaurant. Everything except for the French restaurant was mass scale production. It was here I met Pete Fleming and Ian Cullen, two chefs who had worked at the Gleneagles, Scotland. They were always immaculately dressed and ran the Kitchen with great respect and authority. Pete taught me how to carry myself in a kitchen and work in an organised way. I respected these guys and enjoyed working under them. The basic food preparation skills gave me a good start. I also worked front of house in the banquet suite and bar, under Jean Freestone. I was given loads of shifts and I enjoyed all the work undertaken. Pete and Ian advised me to work hard and to get the position at Claridges.

I had completed a two year General Catering course, and work placement set up by a young lecturer Dave Bolton at 'Claridges Hotel' under chef de cuisine Marjan Lesnik. The pleasant people of my work placement soon became a distant memory. These same people now had a much different attitude towards me. I had to adapt to this reality and quick. When I was offered the post I was hoping this was going to be a dream cooking experience. I was struggling to get on with any of the cooks of authority, which doesn't help when they have the power in such a large kitchen. Its all about team work. This was demonstrated and reinforced by the duties I was given, mainly donkey work! Even the lad I went to college with, Ian, switched on me. I refused to take any rubbish and was swiftly demoted. For the first two months I was put on fruit salad and petit four service. I was not shown that much. Here I was, thinking I was not even good enough to do the donkey work. That was, until Theresa Burrows arrived. It was great having someone teaching you without trying to belittle you, but there was no-one who could save me from the problems I had caused myself through just trying to hold my own. Claridges was a classic kitchen, a large brigade of over 14 pastry cooks and around 80 cooks in the main kitchen. My duties included preparing trays and tray of choux buns and éclairs; these were used for afternoon teas and the sweet trolley. The Afternoon Tea pastries we prepared were fresh fruit tarts, scones, Madeira and fruit cake, lemon meringue, coffee and chocolate éclairs. I also made various compotes of fruits, sorbets with mountains of fresh fruits such as mangoes, squeezing hundreds of lemons, trays of raspberries, the litres of Sauce Anglaise for vanilla ice cream. For the sweet trolley, I made Sherry Trifle, Rum Baba, Crème Caramel and Brûlée, fresh fruit Bavarois, Chocolate Mousse and Pate Sable and Feuilletage. Theresa taught me the basics of pastry. I requested a move into the main kitchen but my pastry chef Michel Guiorel told me "when it came to the vote not one out of the 5 sous chefs running the kitchens would allow me in". I was politely sacked!

This left me not only without a job, but also homeless. So for the next month I ended up sleeping on the floor of four friends I had been to college with. These were Graham Baguley, Ian White, Gary Edson and Jeremy Griffith. Claridges was not all bad! I saw a lot and gained a lot of experience. I mean it was one of the top hotels in the world at those times. The hours of work were straight shifts,. You were paid overtime and you had every other weekend off. **BLISS!!!** The down side to working in such a large kitchen was the fact that it was full of pretenders. You could work there for five years and still not be able to cook. (There are a lot of places to hide in a kitchen with over a hundred cooks.) However, it was a good experience which introduced me to exotic fruits, quality ingredients like truffles, caviar, foie gras, morels and cepes.

I decided that in a large kitchen I was not going to get that 'hands' on part of cookery that I felt my career needed. Jason Wearn, a cook that I would later work with on another two occasions, was the demi chef de partie on the sauce section at 'Claridges'. He told me of a position at a Restaurant in Notting Hill Gate called 'Hills'. The restaurant was owned by an interior designer and the head Chef was Duncan Wallace who had just moved up from sous chef at the 'Capital Hotel', Knightsbridge. It was Jason who basically got me the position at 'Hills'.

It was not a busy restaurant, just trying to find its feet, no big name celebrity chef. A food critic from the Evening Standard gave the restaurant a slating in her column which was the beginning of the end for Duncan at 'Hills'. At this stage there is a slight twist to the story.

Because of a slow and well plotted set up, Duncan's Sous Chef, John (I can't remember his second name) started bad mouthing Duncan off to the owners. On his return they started putting the pressure and work load on Duncan. Even though I had not much experience cooking at this level, I rose to the situation and for the first time under pressure Duncan saw that I was serious about cooking. So even under all his stresses, he was still prepared to teach me. Thank you Duncan! The Sous Chef John walked out and at the time. Duncan and the rest of the team thought that was that. Except the owners actually sacked Duncan! Next day, ex-sous chef John returned on the owner's request, and he and Jason announced that they were going to control the Kitchen. I worked there for a further week or so, just enough time to see the full plot exposed on Duncan's sacking. I was not prepared to work under those conditions so I left. Still in contact with Duncan, he thanked me for sticking by him. He then told me that he could get me a job working for a chef called Brian Turner.

It was Easter week, 1989 and I was going back to Nottingham to see my girlfriend. Duncan rang Mark Clayton (head chef at 'Turners') at 11 o'clock Friday morning. So dressed in ripped jeans and looking kind of rough (not much has changed their then!) I turned up at 'Turners' Restaurant, was given a job and started the following Tuesday.

Brian Turner's name was on the outside of the Walton Street Knightsbridge London double fronted Restaurant. This blue and grey building was to greet me every morning for the next year. The restaurant was a 52 seater, with a small kitchen divided into two main sections. These were the hot range with the service area and the main preparation area which included the sauce section, the pastry section and the pot wash. Brian Turner was on holiday at the time so when I started on the Tuesday, I think he was disappointed that Mark had filled a position without him being there to make the overall decision. Brian didn't speak to me for a few weeks but it didn't bother me. I was in a kitchen that was busy, only had one or two cooks on each section and in order to stay you had to be able to cook. There was no one to blame but yourself, if it did go wrong. It was the best cooking year of my life.

My time keeping was not brilliant, I was consistently late. It reached a stage where Mark Clayton would give me an early morning call! I was living in Walthamstow, a bus and a tube train journey away. It took about an hour to get in and an hour to get home. I lived with a group of fellow caterers, we would all get home around 1am. I wouldn't get to bed until around 3 to 3.30am, (Hey, I was only 19 years old!). I'd start work at 8-9am and finish at around 12am on split shifts. Mark's reasoning for this was to maintain consistency! I wasn't to sure about that! I entered the Kitchen at a stage where most of the cooks had been working there for over a year. Staff there were ready to move to cooking kitchens new. Unknown would-be chefs would arrive late or would not turn up at all. We were always short staffed. I suppose this was due to the long hours, hard work and low pay which gave the catering trade such a high staff turnover. This was the norm and not the exception.

I worked with a lot of ex 'Capital Hotel' staff whilst at 'Turners' (Mr Turner was Executive Chef at the Capital), this had shown me Mr. Turners true managerial skills. My time at 'Turners' saw me work with Jason Wearn and Duncan Wallace although not at the same time.

I was stationed in the larder section. This was the storeroom for food. On this section we carried out butchery, fish, vegetables and starter preparation. First thing in the morning, and the key members had not shown up. I would start the bread dough which was made the previous day and left to prove under refrigeration slowly. To do this, meant weighing out and shaping the dough, then proving it above the range. As it started to warm up it would then be ready to bake by the time the ovens were up to full temperature, freshly baked for lunch service.

At Turners I made a salad of quail which was boned and stuffed with chicken mousse, fines herbs and red peppercorns and rolled into a thin cylindrical shape then gently poached in chicken stock. This was refrigerated until cold then cut at an angle and served on top of a bed of seasoned Belgian chicory, sliced and placed in a ring and served with mixed peppercorn vinaigrette. Mark Clayton cooked a breast of duck which was sealed and pan roasted served with a lamb jus which was sweet and syrupy flavoured with crème de cassis combination of different textures and tastes was to me perfection, yes beautiful. This is why, when this dish was on order, we would grab the sauce pan before it made it to the pot wash with our chunks of bread. This dish, no matter what style of food I was cooking, was going on my own restaurant menu, I knew this, and it did. Another dish which is to this day (because I'm a simple man, enjoying simple flavours) one of my all time favourites is the caramelized individual apple tart. This was apples peeled and cored, sliced thinly on a disk of freshly made puff pastry with a small dollop of pastry cream served with a rich sauce anglaise, garnished with blueberries and a generous dusting of icing sugar. I felt the sauces complimented dishes and made the food complete when on the plate.

I sometimes think a very high standard of professional cooking is worth all the heartache, just to see the finished results of the hours of preparation coming to together. Knowing that, was what made the dishes come alive and work. There were other occasions when things didn't always go to plan. I was ordered by Duncan Wallace not to touch or attempt to prepare the fish which involved filleting a sea bass of gigantic proportions, 6 -8 pounds. I had watch this simple enough procedure done by others on many occasions before, but they had practiced over years. I preceded the words of Duncan going through my mind not to attempt it. I started slowly cutting along the fish. In an instant I had cut right through the bone and ruined a few portions, of what was at the time, one of the most expensive fish on the market. It was at this stage Brian Turner saw me, and shouted for me to STOP! Explaining that he would show me how to do it properly, and any other cooking techniques I wanted to learn!

This was the best cooking year of my life. The kitchen allowed hands on experience and the dish you served was down to you, no one else. Nowhere to hide, and I thoroughly enjoyed it and learned restaurant-style cooking at its fast, furious and hectic pace. I had worked at 'Turners' for a year to the day when I decided that it was time to leave.

So just as I had arrived, Mr. Turner was on holiday. I thought it only appropriate to leave as I had entered, while he was away. Mark Clayton suggested that I should travel to Castle Taunton, Somerset to work with Gary Rhodes. I've got to say at the time I would love to have gone and worked for Gary but I'm glad I didn't because a few months later, he moved back to London to 'The Greenhouse' in Mayfair. I would like to have worked for Gary because I think he is a great cook and his style of cooking is simple but built up to an interesting range of flavours. When you watch his cookery programmes, you learn new cooking skills, no gimmicks. I prefer to watch educational cooking shows such as Gordon

Ramsey's Passion for Flavours. I feel he is original in the type of shows he makes with Delia Smith, Hugh Fearnley-Whittingstall and John Burton Race.

At this stage I decided to go and work for Anthony Worrall Thompson who had just sold the 'Ménage a trois' and was going to open '190 Queensgate'. Whilst waiting for the completion of the deal, I would work at 'KWT' food factory which was an outside catering service, another of Anthony's establishments. This was interesting as I got to do some wealthy outside catering parties at houses in Belgravia, Roy Ackerman's in Chelsea and the largest function we did, was for Marty Wilde's 50th Birthday party at his house. There we had to serve hundreds of half lobster salad, vegetable terrines, Foie Gras and Caviar canapé. This was topped off with a large Birthday cake made in the shape of a guitar.

The function I found the most memorable was one held at 'Le Gavroche'. This was a charity evening with 5 courses selected by five chefs: Anthony Worrall Thompson, Richard Smith, Raymond Blanc, Albert Roux and John King. I had made the starter which was a meaty seafood consommé which set like a rock pool and it went down very well. It then came to cooking the Red mullet from the menu. Richard Smith had not removed the bones. Albert Roux announced "this is the 'le gavroche'; we do not serve any mullet with bones here." There was a mad panic and out of all the cooks there, I was the only one who came prepared with pliers! I was pulling them out like a pro. Worrall Thompson just smiled. Raymond Blanc's dish was Asparagus tips with stuffed Morels, a nightmare to serve because you could only dress four plates at a time. It was the first time I saw Blanc in action. He had with him Richard Neat, who was a very good cook, so Patrick Woodside told me. The Lamb from the 'Le Gavroche' went well. The dessert was prepared by the 'Ritz Hotels' John King, Poire en Cage, this was a poached pear covered with a delicate sugar cage. They didn't want anyone to go near it, but this was a chance to enjoy myself in a 3 star Michelin kitchen, so I did.

Shortly after this, I made what seemed at the time, a rash decision and left 'KWT'. It seemed like forever to sort the '190' deal out but in time I realised that I had made a hasty decision and sometimes Restaurant deals, don't run so smooth .

I then took a few months out, cooking at different Restaurants for no pay. One afternoon there was a cookery programme with Marco Pierre White at Harvey's Restaurant. I saw a familiar face. A chef called Patrick was running the pastry section, I saw Patrick preparing food in a small terraced house Kitchen for my aunts Wedding, I could not believe so much food with so many different flavours could be produced by one man in such a short space of time. That was the first time I realised I was watching a GREAT CHEF in action, Haute Cuisine coming out of the terraces. I called the restaurant and arranged to meet him there. I met Marco for the first time and went to Patrick's house. Patrick was the most influential person in my cooking profession. He gave me advice and guidance on a number of my catering moves. I would visit Patrick fairly regular at Harvey's. I was at the Restaurant the night it was awarded its 2 Michelin stars. The only dish I can remember was Braised Pig Trotters! It was around 1.30am. The cooks had just had a busy service and were now doing mis en place for the lunch service that day. Marco was welcoming on most occasions. I would spend time in the Harvey's kitchens watching preparation. Marco would talk about other chefs, especially ones who I had worked with, and also about some of his cooking techniques. I saw such dishes as the Lemon Tart, the Terrine of leek and langoustine, a chocolate Terrine and Apple Soufflé. It was great to see the quality coming out of such a small awkward kitchen. The pastry section finished in a triangular point with a small confection oven and the area where Marco cooked was near these electric sliding doors out into the restaurant. I had meetings with Patrick in such Kitchens as Harvey's, the Savoy, Tante Claire and Cavaliers. I can remember going to L'Ortolan, Shinfield in a spilt and meeting John Burton Race. He showed me around his restaurant and gave me a sandwich as I mentioned Patrick's name. The last time I met up with Patrick was at his own restaurant which was based in Maddox Street, Soho. Patrick's words of wisdom kept me motivated, even though I never worked with him. Out of all the cooks that I've met out their, past and present, he is in my personal opinion the best cook I have ever met. I suppose that's what life and food is about, opinions and interpretation.

My first meeting with David Cavalier was through Patrick. I was in between jobs after believing nothing was happening for me under Anthony Worrall Thompson. David gave me a position in his kitchen on the vegetable section. Before I took up my post, I was invited to lunch. My timing was slightly out and I got to the restaurant late, (nothing new there!) All the cooks were waiting for us. As professional cooks go they started the meal with a amuses quelle of Wild mushroom Terrine, this was followed by a warm picture perfect salad of langoustine, the salad was very lightly seasoned with hazelnut oil, the langoustines were lightly pan roasted then sprinkled over with balsamic vinegar, topped with toasted pine kernels. The salad was beautiful, the memory of the flavours of this dish gets the juices going all these years on. For the main course we had a sweetbread dish, which I like greatly depending on how it's cooked. I knew I was going to have problems as it was braised. This reminded me of a chicken dish my grand mother cooked when I was about 8 with the skin still on and I didn't like it. The texture was in my memory bank and as soon as I had my first mouthful, my taste buds just shut down. We could not be disrespectful, so discretely, we wrapped it in a napkin and put it in Tracey's bag! We ate all the vegetable and sauce which was very well cooked and presented. For Dessert Patrick prepared a hot strawberry soufflé with a small tuile of fresh berries and lemon sorbet served with a fruit coulis, this to was perfection on a plate. After a great meal, I was looking forward to working at Cavaliers Restaurant and one of my first jobs on my to do list was change the way David cooked the sweetbreads. This was to make them crispier on the outside and they melted in the mouth on the inside when you ate them. I enjoyed preparing the Foie Gras Terrine served with a Beaume de Venise jelly, a very simple dish which had great flavour.

Cavaliers was the quietest restaurant that I had worked in but all this was made up for by the precise level of the work put into preparation of ingredients. Everything had to be perfect and consistent. Pure concentration was needed when it came to preparing baton and turned carrots measuring each one to be sure. There was a potato dish pomme sarladaise which I had to prepare and served with a Barbary Duck. It was a bit of a nightmare. It had two different sized circles that were placed in a 2 ½ inch diameter mould, placing a little duck fat in the mould, taking the smallest roundel and cutting it around 2mm thick, placing one in the centre and then fanning the rest on the outside using around eight slices. Then taking the second circle which was slightly smaller than the mould and cutting them around 3mm thick, placing the first layer on top of the first layer of garlic puree then the next layer. Once to the top it was then covered with foil and then baked. It was a difficult dish because it was very easy to burn. You could only prepare one at a time and they also had to be made around 20 minutes before service, so there was no room for error. Looking back at it

Cavaliers; when you did 10 or 20 covers, was the equivalent of serving 30-60 covers at Turners. I respected David cooking and methods, his style was at the time modern, very trendy and technical. Each individual dish was like a full menu all on its own. I'm glad to say that I worked at Cavaliers the year it was awarded its Michelin star and through the busiest time of the year, November and December months. I learnt to produce precision quality under pressure day in, day out, so I knew during my training days I had succeeded the hardest challenge in the kitchen, working with a very temperamental chef who was aiming to have a big reputation in the cooking game. He was definitely good enough. David Cavalier never really told me how good my cooking was but it was obviously improving because week by week, month by month, my barracking became fewer and fewer. He would ask my opinion on certain dishes to be put on the menu. I was getting on far better with all the other cooks which at this level of cooking, was always a good sign. I worked hard and tried to learn as much has I could. David's cookery had a lot of influences from Nico Ladenis and Anton Mosimann so the application of cooking and presentation was very precise. I enjoyed my stint at Cavaliers and would have liked to have completed a few more months, but that's how it go sometimes. I eventually left 'Cavaliers' after a small petty dispute. I did not want to leave but in those days my word was my bond.

While in between jobs I started working at a catering agency. I would earn enough money to cover my bills. I would then get in contact with the top kitchens in the country and work there for no pay. Patrick had encouraged me to try for a job at Le Manoir aux Quat Saison. He told me not to mention his name to Raymond Blanc. When Raymond saw me he said "For a minute there I thought Patrick was back in the Kitchen." I played dumb and just laughed. The Head Chefs name was Clive Fretwell. I went for a few days, and was then asked to go back for a working interview. They provided my accommodation and meals. I stayed for two and a half weeks. It was a brilliant cooking experience. The setting of Le Manoir was idyllic. It had stables with horses and tennis courts which I played on with other chefs in my split. It also had its own vegetable and herb gardens. I remember during a lunch time service, the section I was working on ran out of salad. I was asked by the chef de partie to go and pick a selection of continental lettuces. Within 5 minutes the salad was being seasoned and served in the restaurant. Now that is what I call fresh! Raymond Blancs kitchen was staffed with loads of cooks who had been head chefs at other Hotels and restaurants. Raymond Blanc's kitchen made me really appreciate the work and preparation that was put in to produce such quality food, using quality ingredients. He also liked cooking in natural juices and making light sauce. He would protect meats by taking the first layer of skin and re-wrapping it around, such as lamb fillet. I worked in all the sections, preparing such dishes as the menu gourmand. This was new to me; it was a selection of around seven courses, from different areas of the original menu.

At the end of my interview I had to cook a dish for Raymond Blanc. It was his Sunday lunch. I decided to cook a Pan Fried Sea bass with a Salad of baby vegetables and citrus vinaigrette. He ate the dish and liked the way I had cooked the fish which was a la Turners. He then said "I think you have just got yourself a job here". I waited for two weeks, only to receive a letter saying I had not got the post. He must have found out that I was connected to Patrick.

I went to Michel Rouxs 3 Star Waterside Inn, Bray on Thames. Head Chef was Mark Dodd. I was there for about 10 days. This was classical French cookery at its very best. I was placed on the sauce section and worked with a commis chef called Philip Cooper. I prepared stocks and garnishes for the large range of meat dishes. I was asked by the chef de partie to prepare a julienne of oranges for some marmalade, it was a whole box. I swear it was a nightmare. It took me about three or four hours. My hands were killing me, the chef de partie just laughed. I remember it being a friendly kitchen and Michel Roux would cover a lot of the service. I enjoyed it there. There was a waiting list to start work of about 6 months. I could not wait that long so I applied for a job two weeks later at Les Allouettes. I went for an interview on the Friday and on the Saturday I received a letter from the Waterside Inn offering me the post of commis chef starting immediately. I had to turn it down as I had already accepted Les Allouettes an, as usual, my word was my bond. Mistake!

I tried to get into Nico Ladenis Simply Nico to work for no pay but he didn't offer that service. I had written to Nico a few months before and I was quite impressed because Nico sent me a hand written letter of rejection. I think I still have it some where.

I moved to Les Allouettes. This restaurant was totally different to Cavaliers. Cavaliers had a modern trendy cooking style in keeping with my thinking and Les Allouettes was more strong classic French cooking. The cooking at Cavaliers was the best I had ever done.. This heavier Classical French cooking, it wasn't for me. I knew I had made a mistake, I had earned my respect at Cavaliers, and he had earned mine, even if it was never said. Now I was in a kitchen where in time I realised it's not all about reputation because Michel Perraud had one, he had been head chef at the Waterside Inn for a number of years. As a man I did not rate or respect him, me a novice commis chef with around three years experience. I knew I had made a big mistake; I had turned down a position at the three star Michelin restaurant, the Waterside Inn to work for Michel. Don't get it twisted, I thought he was going to work me like a dog. He didn't but he tried to treat me like one. I was the only Black and British person in the entire building, the rest were French. I first had to get over that obstacle. That was because I wanted to learn French and they wanted to speak English. I got on well with all of the staff except for the Chef and that wasn't good. The dishes on the menu were heavy cream of asparagus or mushroom soup, Chauterbriand with a red wine sauce; Dover sole with a fish mousseline, vegetables served on a crescent shaped dish with a puree of the day, I thought it was messy and went against all I was starting to believe in. I wanted out! I worked on the Vegetable section but like any competitive kitchen I wanted to step up, especially being as young and hungry as I was! After a few months I moved onto the larder section at the expense of a young lad called Neness. Michel packed him of to London. He didn't stand a chance!

The Lobster Bisque was one of the dishes I prepared off the menu. It was full of strong individual flavour, coming together to make a wonderful starter. The Lobster Terrine was a time consuming dish to make, taking the raw lobster meat, and pureeing it, passing it through a sieve and then cooling it, adding egg whites then gradually add the double cream on a bed of ice. The mousse was tested for correct texture. You did this by cooking a small amount in a steamer or placing it in hot water. The pancakes were then prepared. These were made with Pernod and fines herbes. They were then used to line the Terrine. It was then built up with poached lobster, blanched carrots and French beans covered in cling film and foil baked in a bain-marie in the oven. This was then cooled at room temperature, refrigerated with a weight placed on top. It was served warm with a tomato butter sauce. I must say, the first time I made this dish was with Neness. We were messing about a bit and got the recipe slightly wrong. Too much cream was added. Michel did not like waste, so he made us pay for the ingredient and remake the dish.

I got a lot of hassle. I felt that Michel Perraud was trying to break me like back in the early days but I was having none of it!. I weighed up the whole situation. The food I was cooking wasn't all that! and if I was going to put up with his rubbish six days a week, he'd have to step up his level of cooking and stop victimizing this so called weak person in his Kitchen. All his sly dirty tricks were not going to break me. I can understand not telling me about special parties and functions once, but not once a week, and the pay was not great. I'd had enough; I decided to leave 'Les Allouettes'.

There was a French bakery which delivered bread to 'Les Allouettes', which was owned by Philipe Dade. I wanted to work there as they had become friends. I was given a job at the bakery with a catch. Before I could start I had to do an extra month at Perrauds. That was not too bad as when you know you're on the way out, the last month at 'Les Allouettes' did not seem that bad and I did enjoy my time working and living with the French. It was a shame Michel got me there under false pretences but as I grew older I soon realised that this was just life.

My first day at 'Boulangerie patisserie Dade' was a Nightmare, not only was it a new job, I had decided to changed my ways and I arrived at work early. Big mistake!
The place was like a bomb had hit it. All the other staff were over an hour late and it took a further hour to sort ourselves out. I found that it was the most disorganised kitchen I had ever worked in. I was put on the viennoiserie section making croissants and Danish pastry. Fortunately for myself and people working with me, I had worked in a bakery in South London part/ time with a baker by the name of John Panice. This was also making croissants and Danish Pastries, I was moonlighting when. London was an expensive place to live then and still is now let me tell you. It was on the same estate as KWT. However, I never told Anthony this.

The Second chef Yvon Connaird, he was forever running off and sorting out other things, which to me, did not concern him. Therefore, because of this, each day we would lose about two / three hours on production time. Also instead of him just allowing us to have a method of production, he preferred us to just do the hours. Again, I was thinking about jacking in the job and for once I had not given anybody my word. Then one afternoon he disappeared for a while so I just jumped on the machine, the pastry break and started producing the works. Yvon did not say a word, and over the next few weeks my aim was to produce all the workload by 5 o'clock instead of 9, 10 and 11 o'clock. I'm serious!

A baker then came on to run the section, Theirry, but by this times I was getting a bit of an attitude. That's because everyone was trying to be the boss but this was a section where there was no head man. It was just about getting the job done and working as an organised team. When things were not going my way, I would not talk to the people who were not holding their own and argued with the people in charge. It was not about position or age, it was just you respect me and I'll respect you and vice/versa. I'm on that score now. The same person, but in many other ways a changed man.

Back to Dade's. Within two and a half months the section was finishing the work by three thirty and that was kitchen and section scrubbed down. After finishing on that section I would the go and work with Alain Ronez. He was an excellent pastry chef, with a wealth of experience and knowledge but allowed lads that in my opinion were not as good as him, in the form of Philippe and Yvon to take the piss. Alain should have gone it alone years ago in the kitchen. He was hard but fair, and I think that's why Alain and I got on so well, or it could have been the fact I gave him a lift home each night. I did not get on with Philippe Dade. However, at the end of the day, I believe he knew who got his day time Kitchen in order. I was there to do a job and that job was done! He would come into the kitchen ranting and raving, but when it was on top I would shout my point across in positions which I really and truly should have been sacked for. However, like I say, he knew what was what in his Kitchen, and knew that what ever, I was producing the goods.

The method I used to make the croissants, French strong flour and quality French unsalted butter, produced the best I have ever tasted. The dough was made the night before, with trimmings from the previous batch added to the freshly made dough. In the morning my first job was to soften the butter, cut, and weigh the dough, around 4 kilos. I would then mould it, place the butter into the dough, it would then be flattened to fit through the pastry brake. The dough would be turned one single turn, rested then a double turn. Three batons were placed on a tray wrapped in half a bin liner so not to form a skin. 10-15 trays would be put on the trolley and each baton would produce around 120 croissants which when baked had a rich, light, leafy layered, well coloured croissant which just melted in your mouth. Nice! The pain au chocolat and almond croissants were the best I have ever tasted and enjoyed reproducing these items for my own customers. Boulangerie Dades was situated on an industrial estate not too far from Wembley. It was a large kitchen with three main areas. The Head baker Jean Louis was a brilliant baker' he work that hard and such long hours that he looked like a zombie and worked like a mad man, consistently producing the best Continental bread in London. When he wasn't working he was sleeping. He had worked in London 8 months and had not seen any of the great sites of London. Damn shame! In the centre of the kitchen was the pastry area. Alain Ronez worked this section, working day in, day out producing quality goods. Then came my section, this was a good size and was where all the pastry goods were baked.

I stayed at the bakery for around nine months, then I was making my way back to Nottingham but I first made one last stop to work in a bakery in Balham with an old friend John Panice. I was there for about three month and got into a few heated arguments, to me, John was not the type of man to do battle with in those days. This is when I decided to quit London and moved to work towards setting up my own business, and returned to Nottingham.

I had no money, so decided to take a job working nights in an Italian bakery. I was earning less money at the age of 22 than when I was 16 but it wasn't about the money it was about knowledge. I believed the money would come later (I'm still waiting). I worked there for just under a year, having the piss taken out of me once again, but the only thing was this chap was polite with it so it was acceptable and I was learning things new. Whilst working at the bakery I had a part/time position working at a Residential home. That was different, but in changing from the London to my home town, the attitudes to work were completely different. Everyone in London I had worked with, just wanted to work hard and get on and to the top of their chosen career but in Nottingham it was more about getting paid and less about job satisfaction. From the bakery, I went to work at John Players. 'Yeah that's right, the cigarette factory' as a pastry cook, honest! I was in between jobs while saving and applying for funding to set up my own pastry manufacturing unit.

All my training in and around London put me in good stead to tackle my personal challenge which I set at the age of sixteen. When others were still figuring out what they wanted to do, my thoughts were so clear. I could visualise my future working for myself. At 23 years old, I went in search of premises all over Nottinghamshire. For months I searched. I then came across a shop in Radford, half a mile from where I grew up and spent my early childhood. The location was where in 1981 the riots had taken place, not as high profile as Toxteth and Brixton but it was if you were living there and I was. The premises were rooted in the inner city, the concrete jungle where there was the highest unemployment rate and people claiming benefits in Nottingham. Although 200 yards over the road was the richest area in the city, The Park Estate, situated near the castle. Radford a wrong-doers paradise, a criminal's oasis. It's very close to the red light district, where prostitutes, violent street robbers, drug dealers, burglars and shop lifters worked and lived and not through choice. I suppose victims them selves of situations and circumstances, their options and opportunities shut down.

As I was setting up a pastry manufacturing unit, I just needed a kitchen with a good amount of space. La Maison Rouge Patisserie Continental was born! I had to rely on no one. The whole kitchen was my responsibility. The proverbial buck stops here!

I had made a whole range of desserts and developed new recipes based on my own experience: Gateaux, Tarts, flans, meringues, tortes and roulades. All manner of Danish pastries flowed from my kitchen. The use of chocolate, the world's favourite aphrodisiac, was mixed, laced, with all sorts of liquors, rums, whiskeys, brandy and sherry's. A distillery would have been proud of the optimum usage of their most sort after product. Once finished, I was satisfied enough for it to adorn any restaurant table. I had set my stall for anyone to try my ware and pass judgement. My range was extensive now. I had to look for customers. All the time I was researching, trying to improve whether it was presentation, down to the glaze finish on the citron mousse, or the apricot glaze to protect and preserve the freshest of fruit on the tarts or did my apple tart really appeal to the nakedness of the eye, was it enough?

At the age of 23 I had fulfilled the ambitions I had put down as a young innocent 16 years old, to run and establish my own business. I had never been promoted or held a senior position in a kitchen in my whole career and here I was running and doing my own thing. Scary!

I travelled to London once again and scouted around, looking in Patisseries shops and the food halls of Harrods, just to make sure that being so isolated in Nottingham my own standards and judgement were not slipping. Being a professional cook, preparing food for other peoples pleasure it was a life times task to educate my palate so others would benefit. My working practise meant late nights, little sleep and while normal people were out on the street enjoying themselves, I was trapped inside my self made prison in which I had sentenced my self most of the time to solitary confinement with regular visits from family and friends. But as soon as they stepped through the door, they had volunteered to wash pots, weigh ingredients and generally help out.

While everyone was out partying I had an appointment with hundreds and hundreds of eggs, kilos of sugar and flour, turning them into Genoise sponge. Out on the streets would be a commotion and police and ambulance sirens flashing blue lights, senseless, gratuitous, street crime. You know the type of stuff you read about. Well, I was living in it with my limited thoughts. My car was damaged and broken into over 15 times in just as many months. Living in such poverty stricken environment makes you take desperate chances which can no doubt change your whole life.

The late night means many things to different people. In my kitchen all this meant to me was deadlines! Thursday, Friday and Saturday was when the work really came in. Totally different from restaurant cooking. No matter how much preparation was done, I was a condemned man. Waking up at 3 am Thursday morning, working until 9pm, sleeping until 12am Friday morning, working until 7pm, sleeping until 10pm, then working through until 6pm Saturday evening. The longest straight shift I ever worked was 37 hours. It was torture. Sleep deprivation is not nice, especially when it's your own creation. I suppose that's what separates those cooking for pleasure from those cooking for profession.

I would not recommend this approach to anyone, only those who are serious. This is all about food. I was in the heart of the inner city. Nottingham had no international reputation. I was a million miles away from Michelin restaurants, but all the practical knowledge was there imprinted. How to order, what to prepare, how to stay on top whilst being true to the profession of flavour, textures and fundamentally taste. My taste buds were like a finely tuned instrument, everything had its place. The food was just consistency itself, every day I would fight to master the art of food.

Thousands of eggs were cracked; flour and sugar were whisked and beaten. You develop a relationship with certain basic ingredients that will keep the bank manager and all the other loan sharks at bay. Small businesses are notorious for drowning, going under and so keeping my head above water was my continuing permanent concerns. I couldn't possibly forget all my influential teaching gained from Claridges, Turners, Cavaliers and Boulangerie Patisserie Dade. Vital knowledge was gained from brief encounters at such places as The Waterside Inn, Le Gavroche, Harvey's and La Manoir aux Quat Saison all teaching the importance of good preparation, taste and quality attention to detail and presentation.

Rooted in the Inner City my book talks exclusively of my past. I don't have to make any excuse for my food and the results. Tastes and flavours do matter as you well know. Food is one of the greatest negotiators. A poor man, like myself, with a little knowledge can prepare and produce food fit for a king and at every meal time eat like one.

Seasonings are meant to enhance the food, but you have to work constantly with food to make it taste as it should and when it does then it's a question of knowing when to stop. When creating dishes it's best to go to the freshest quality producer, and then build the recipe from fresh. I would go down to a farm to pick my own fresh raspberries, buy local organic eggs, add sugar, flour and cocoa powder. I would produced a rich chocolate sponge soaked in stock syrup flavoured with Kirsch, covered in a creamy rich bitter chocolate ganache, that's what I would call a bitter sweet chocolate heaven. A Strawberry gateau I produced would promise and deliver the exact amount of morishness necessary for the palate. A cook is always looking to challenge himself, tasting and creating simple dishes

Running 'La Maison Rouge Patisserie Continentals' was hard, because when people said 'yes' to doing business with me, they meant 'no' (I really felt their decision financially). It took me about two weeks to get my first order, eight chocolate and hazelnut gateaux and one hundred fresh fruit tarts and it took me ages to complete the order. I can remember thinking this was going to be a long hard ride. The 'Gateway Hotel' kept me in business for the first three weeks. I then met the sous chef from Newcastle. He, for some strange reason took a disliking to me and I lost that order. It was then I took to the phones.

A hotel I had worked for at 17 gave me the golden call! They wanted Gateau St Honore for one hundred people. That evening Graham Baguley and I worked through the night burning our fingers, the order went well and the 'Royal Moathouse' and it's sister hotel the 'Nottingham Moathouse' insured my new business stayed afloat for the next four and a half years guaranteed. So thank you and I apologise to all those who took offence to my 'don't give a damn attitude' but it's the only thing that was allowing me to survive or so I believed at the time. In those days don't think just because you were spending money with me I had to change and behave differently like your other suppliers. With my bolshy attitude, I held my own and enjoyed every minute of it, the highs and the lows, the goods and the bad. I believe that's what life is all about and that's what's made me the person I am. The influence of people I came in contact with from birth to present day.

My interest in food has to start with the smell of those simple natural ingredients to transform them into enjoyable dishes well prepared. The basic smell of the kitchen, the simmering of the stock, the roasting of the bones, the traditional proverbial chicken or the roasting various meats, the desserts, the apple tart just cooked drifting over the small airspace of the this small kitchen. The sponge cake made with the freshest eggs, soft flour, the sweetest of sugars and butter beaten so lightly, that it disappears on the tongue on impact. This alone can surely convince anyone of the beauty of food, raw and cooked.

After three and a half years of 'La Maison Rouge' I decided to expand my business by opening a Caribbean sandwich Bar and take away. This held it's own, while I was still making good money from the cakes. I was then asked to go into business partnership on a restaurant where the owner had become very ill and he just wanted rid of it. I entered the restaurant for next to nothing and on the word of my partners I took out extra loans and everything. My partners were getting cold feet but I could see the previous owner under pressure more than myself.. Hence, for his sake not mine, I tried to run the business smoothly. I however, my partner did pull out, and the owner sadly died two months later. I washed my hands of the whole of my business enterprise 'La Maison Rouge', 'Tilly's Take away' and 'Alannah's French /Caribbean Restaurant'. What's in a name, hey?

I worked as a volunteer, organising cookery workshops and training courses throughout Nottingham, working with a cross section of the community with children aged from 5 and adults aged up to 65. I was working for over 4 years, trying to educate inner city residents the benefit of cooking using fresh produce. Working with parents, teaching them to cook healthy nutritious meals, to me was the most rewarding work I had ever carried out. I applied for local government funding, but unfortunately was repeatedly refused. Then I worked part time at New College Nottingham, Entry programme.

The Inner City Caribbean cookbook is practical, comprising of simple recipes to cut down on hours spent in the kitchen whilst still creating wonderfully tasting food with good flavour to keep your friends, family and guests well entertained.

Taking those Caribbean classics and bringing it up to date, with my own personal interpretation, most recipes have been adapted to fit in with the home cooks needs and resources. This book is written with my favourite dishes for you to adapt and make good use of. The quick and easy Breadfruit and Oyster soup, Jerk Chicken Terrine, Braised Oxtail with butterbeans, Roast lobster Bake, Vegetarian Callaloo Soufflé and Ackee Torte, and the beautifully light rich Jamaican Ginger cake, the chocolate lovers dream Triple chocolate mousse flavoured with rum. These are some of the dishes in the Inner city Caribbean cookbook that I enjoy cooking and eating for my friends and family for our dining pleasure.

I personally believe that in order to appreciate the recipes in my book, you must have a little knowledge of cooking to get a true understanding of the recipes. I am not going to preach what you should and shouldn't do with this book. This is just a rough guideline for recipes that work. The more you attempt them the more you will influence the dish with your personal touch for flavours and textures to suit your palate.

It is some years now since I cooked professionally. I now cook for pleasure, for friends and family. So here it is, the Inner City Caribbean Cookbook. My chance to share a part of my past and present with you.

Enjoy

SOUPS
&
STARTERS

CALLALOO SOUP

PUMPKIN SOUP

ALLIGATOR PEAR SOUP

ACKEE AND CALLALOO TART avocado and tomato salad

BRUL - JOL

TONGA AND ROAST PEPPER SALAD

LOBSTER AND SALTFISH CAKE

BREADFRIUT & OYSTERS SOUP

JAMAICAN TILAPIA SALAD with green banana chips

ESCOVEICITCH FISH

JERK CHICKEN TERRINE

CHICKEN & MANGO SALAD

FISH TEA

CALYPSO GRILLED PIGEON SALAD

SPICY CRAB AND VEGETABLE ROLLS

CALALOO SOUP

(Serves 4)

Calaloo was a vegetable that as a child was an acquired taste, but growing up I learned to like it as I am sure you will.

450g	Callaloo	**Garnish**
25g	Butter	
1 medium	Onion (chopped)	Double Cream
2	Garlic clove (pureed)	Shredded Callaloo
1	Scotch bonnet (finely diced)	
750 ml	Vegetable stock	
1 sprig	Thyme	
250 ml	Coconut milk	
	Salt & Freshly Ground Pepper	

1. If using fresh callaloo, wash leaves in cold salted water. If using tinned then drain before using.
2. Heat the butter in a sauce pan, add the onion, garlic and scotch bonnet, and cook without colour for a few minutes.
3. Pour in the stock and add thyme. Bring to boil, then turn down the heat and simmer for 10 minutes.
4. Add the calaloo and coconut milk, and simmer for a further 10 minutes.
5. Puree the soup with a blender and return to a clean pan, reheat.
6. Add seasoning and adjust consistency if needed by adding more vegetable stock.

Garnish: When serving, pour a little cream into the centre of the soup and add a little shredded callaloo or pureed callaloo.

PUMPKIN SOUP

(Serves 4)

		Garnish
25 g	Butter	
1 medium	Onion (chopped)	
600 g	Pumpkin (diced)	Turned or small balls of
1 medium	Carrot (diced)	Pumpkin ⎤
1 litre	Vegetable stock	Potatoes ⎦ (boiled)
150 g	Potatoes (diced)	
1	Bouquet garni (optional)	
250 ml	Double cream	
	Salt & freshly ground pepper	

1 Heat the saucepan; add the butter, sweat of the onion, pumpkin, and carrot for 5 minutes without colour.
2 Add the vegetable stock, potatoes and bouquet-garni then bring to the boil. Turn down the heat and simmer for a further 20 - 25 minutes.
3 Allow to cool slightly, and then put through a food processor, finally passing through a strainer.
4 Return to clean saucepan, reheat and season.
5 When ready to serve add the cream.

Garnish: When serving add turned or balls of pumpkin, potatoes.

PUMPKIN SOUP

ALLIGATOR PEAR SOUP

(Serves 4)

This soup is very quick and easy to make, and is served cold.

2	Avocado
½ tsp	Scotch bonnet (diced)
1	Lime (Juice)
275 ml	Vegetable stock (BASIC 7)
150 ml	Milk
75 ml	Double cream
	Salt & freshly ground pepper

Garnish

Peeled and diced tomato
Diced Avocado

1   Take the two ripe Avocados, cut in half to remove the stone. Peel off the skin and dice.
2   The Scotch Bonnet should be very finely diced.
3   Place all the ingredients in the blender, and blend until smooth.
4   Check the consistency, pass through a strainer or conical, and season.

Garnish: Dress the diced tomato and avocado in an herb vinaigrette and place on top of the soup.

ALLIGATOR PEAR SOUP

ACKEE & CALLALOO TART
avocado and tomato salad

(Serves 4)

25 g	Butter	**for salad:**
1	Shallot (finely chopped)	
2	Garlic cloves (pureed)	2 tomatoes peeled and diced
125 g	Callaloo (cooked)	1 Avocado
125 g	Ackee	1 Red onion
½ tsp	Nutmeg	Fresh herbs
4	Savoury tarts baked (BASIC 21)	
2	Eggs	
125 ml	Double cream and milk	Citrus vinaigrette (BASIC 11)
25-50 g	Grated cheese	
	Salt & freshly ground pepper	

1   Heat butter in a pan, add the shallots and garlic puree sweat without colour, and take off the heat.
2   Add to this the callaloo; ackee and nutmeg, then leave to cool.
3   Place the baked savoury tart on a tray.
4   Fill the tarts with ackee and the callaloo mix.
5   Mix the egg and cream together, season then fill tarts with egg mix and sprinkle with cheese.
6   Bake in the oven for 8 - 10 minutes at 180C.
7   Add small diced peeled peppers, chopped onions and chopped seasoned tomato to the vinaigrette.

To serve: place the tart in the middle of a plate with the vinaigrette drizzled around.

ACKEE & CALLALOO TART
avocado and tomato salad

BRUL JOL

(Serves 4)

1	Shallot (finely chopped)
50 g	Mixed pepper (small diced)
225 g	Saltfish (cooked and flaked)
½	Juice of lime
4	short crust tartlets (BASIC 21)
2	Escallion
2	Tomatoes (diced)
1	Avocado
100 ml	Vegetable stock
½	Lemon juice
	Salt & freshly ground pepper

Escallion, Tomatoes, Avocado, Vegetable stock, Lemon juice, Salt & freshly ground pepper } Sauce

1. Sweat the shallots and mixed pepper then place into a mixing bowl.
2. Add to this the flaked saltfish, lime juice, mayonnaise and season with pepper.
3. Spoon the mixture into the tartlet case.
4. Take the escallion, tomatoes place in small bowl.
5. In a food processor, add the avocado, vegetable stock and lemon juice and blend well. Pass through a sieve and season. Add to the escallions and tomatoes.
6. Serve the sauce around and over the tart.

TONGA AND ROAST PEPPER SALAD

(Serves 4)

12 - 16	Crayfish (cooked)
2	Tomatoes (chopped)
1	Avocado (chopped)
4	Cho-cho (diced)
2	Escallion (sliced)
150 g	Mayonnaise
1	roast green and yellow pepper
½	Lime (juice)
2	Garlic chopped
25g	Butter
2tbsn	Parsley
	Salt

1   Place the diced tomato, avocado, cho-cho, escallion and mayonnaise in a bowl and bind together, spoon into the centre of the plate.
2   Skinned peel and dice peppers.
3   Heat the butter in a frying pan and add the crayfish, garlic and peppers, sauté for 2 minutes, season and add parley.

LOBSTER & SALTFISH CAKE

(Serves 4)

I love lobster and I like the flavour that salted cod has. You can not get this distinct flavour that I like using fresh cod. This dish can also be made using Tiger or king prawns.

The lobster and saltfish cakes can be made earlier in the day and then cooked to order. These can then be made larger and served for a main course.

600 g	Baking potatoes
1	Egg yolk
25 g	Butter
300 g	Cooked saltfish (flaked)
300 g	Cooked lobster (cut into 1cm pieces)
1 clove	Garlic
1 tsp	Curry powder
2	Escallions (sliced)
	Ground pepper
25 g	Butter
150 g	Hard dough bread crumbs
1	Egg
	Flour for coating and moulding

Spicy tomato and pepper sauce (BASIC 13)

1. Bake the potatoes, scoop out, and mash until smooth into a creamy mix. When cool enough add the egg yolks and butter.
2. Into a bowl place flaked Saltfish and diced lobster and to this add, garlic, curry powder and escallions,

3   Mix gently together then add the potato mix.
4   Season with salt and pepper, then mould into desired shape.
5   Chill, and then pass the shaped potato through flour, then egg, then hard dough bread crumbs. Repeat this to give them a good coating.
6   Shallow fry until golden brown. Approx. 3-4 minutes

Serve with spicy tomato and pepper sauce.

BREADFRUIT & OYSTER SOUP

(Serves 4)

I personally grappled with breadfruits, but my grandfather would just bake it in the oven or put it in an open fire. I really like this dish because the two flavours go really well together, and it is so simple to prepare.

1 whole	Breadfruit (fresh or tinned)
1	Onion (chopped)
125 ml	Coconut milk
125 ml	Double cream
750 g	Vegetable stock
25 g	Butter
4 - 12	Oysters & Juice

Garnish: chopped chives, season sliced tomatoes and cucumber batons

1   Melt the butter in a thick bottomed pan, add the onions and gently cook without colour
2   Peel the breadfruit and cut into small dice. Add the breadfruit to the cooked onion, along with the stock and bring to the boil, turn down heat and simmer for 20 minutes.
3   Add the coconut milk, simmer for 5 minutes, and add the double cream. Check the seasoning to taste.
4   Open the oysters and save the juice

To serve: Place the soup into a bowl, putting the oysters and juice onto the soup and garnish with a little chopped chives, season sliced tomato and thin batons of peeled cucumber.

BREADFRUIT & OYSTER SOUP

JAMAICAN TILAPIA SALAD
with green banana chips

(Serves 4)

4	Fillets of tilapia (prepared)	**Honey Vinaigrette**
	Oil (for deep frying)	
		90 ml Olive oil
2	Green banana	30 ml Honey
4	Tomatoes (blanched)	30 ml White wine
½	Cucumber	or cider vinegar
1	Mango	
1	papaya	
1	red onion	
	Salt & freshly ground pepper	

1 Cut the fillets into 2-3 pieces. Season the fillets with salt and pepper, brush with a little oil.
2 Slice the plantain and green banana very fine, deep fry and drain season with a little salt.
3 Pre heat a baking tray, place the fish under the grill for 5 minutes.
4 While the fish is grilling pack into centre of ring taking the plantain and banana chips and scatter around the plate.
5 Place fish on top of salad and serve.
6 Deseed tomatoes and dice along with cucumber, mango papaya and red onion, leave in a bowl when ready to dress add fresh herb.

Honey vinaigrette: Whisk all the ingredients together and store in a small bottle, shake well before serving.

JAMAICAN TILAPIA SALAD
with green banana chips

ESCOVEICITCH FISH

(Serves 4)

This dish was cooked for me very well by my mother I was not quite old enough to eat this when my grandfather made it, as the preparation of the fish was quite simply scale and gut the fish then cook with everything else in tack. My grandmother would always get bones stuck in her throat. When I eat the whole fish it's eaten very slowly to appreciate flavour's and respect the bones.

6	Snapper (filleted and boned)	**Garnish**
1	Lime (juice)	
4 medium	Onions (sliced)	Lemon Vinaigrette (BASIC 11)
1	Yellow Scotch Bonnet	Turned Cucumber (20)
75 ml	White Wine Vinegar	Blanched Tomato petals (20)
350 ml	Fish Stock	
1 tsp	Fish Seasoning	
	Salt & Freshly Ground Pepper	

1. Season the fish with Lime, Salt and Pepper. Then leave to marinade for 20 - 30 minutes.
2. While the fish is marinating, sweat of the onion and Scotch Bonnet in a sauce pan, add the white wine vinegar and fish stock. Reduce by half.
3. The onions should be transparent and have a sharp peppery flavour.
4. Heat a little olive oil in a non stick frying pan, when hot place fillet flesh side down for 30 seconds, then turn over and cook for 3 minutes or until crisp golden brown.

To serve: Place a 6-7 cms ring in centre of the plate. Add a layer of onions, then add the fillets on top of each other in a stack of three. Place the cucumber and tomato in crosses around the plate and drizzle cooking liquor over the fish.

ESCOVEICITCH FISH

JERK CHICKEN TERRINE

(Serves 4)

I served this dish in my restaurant. It went down well, with the delicate light flavoured mousse and combined with the succulent breast of chicken the fierce heat from the jerk seasoning makes a fantastic combination.

4	Chicken Breast	
	Chicken Seasoning	
1	Egg	
Good pinch	Salt	
Pinch	Cayenne pepper	Mousse
225ml	Chilled Double Cream	
6	Breasts of Chicken	
	Jerk Seasoning (BASIC 18)	
	Calaloo	

1 Chop the four chicken breasts into large dices, and then put into the food processor and blend on pulse until smooth. Scrape down the sides.
2 Add to this the salt and egg, then refrigerated for 30mins- 1hr.
3 Add to the chicken whilst in the processor, the cayenne pepper, and chilled cream gradually on pulse, slowly until you have a smooth paste.
4 Keep refrigerate until ready to use.
5 Marinade the remaining six chicken breasts for 2 hours in jerk seasoning then bake for 20 minutes in pre-heated oven gas 6, 200C, 400F.
6 Butter and line a terrine (1 kg loaf tin) with two layers of cling film, over lapping.
7 Take the large leaves of calaloo and line the terrine mould.
8 Place a layer of chicken mousse in the mould.
9 Then place a layer of chicken breast.
10 Add another layer of mousse then add more chicken breasts.
11 Now add the last layer of mousse then fold in the callaloo leaves to cover the top.
12 Cover with cling film and then tin foil.

13 Bake for 40 - 50 minutes in a tray of water at gas mark 3, 170C, 330F.

14 Leave to cool, then refrigerate until ready to serve

Serve: warm with a light creamy yogurt sauce (Basic 29).

CHICKEN AND MANGO SALAD

(Serves 4)

		Marinade	
2 x 225g	Breast of chicken	½	Lemon
1	Mango (large))	1 clove	Garlic
150 ml	Mayonnaise	1 tsp	Thyme
1 tbsp	Tarragon (chopped)	1	Shallots (chopped)
100 ml	Chicken stock	1 tsp	Parsley
4	Tomatoes (blanched)	½	Scotch bonnet
1	Small red onion	2 tsp	Ginger
1	Cucumber (peeled)	3 seeds	Allspice
		25 ml	Olive oil

1 Prepare the marinade by crushing in a pestle and mortar to blend. Marinade the chicken breasts for 2 hours.
2 Prepare the mango by peeling and deseeding.
3 Place half the Mango into a blender and puree, then place into a bowl, add the mayonnaise and tarragon, and use some of the chicken stock to thin down the sauce, and then refrigerate.
4 Dice the onion, remove seed and dice the tomatoes, peel the cucumber and dice the remaining mango.
5 Grill the chicken for 8-10 minutes.
6 To serve, place the salad leaves in the centre of the plate alternate the chicken and mango salad coat with mango mayonnaise.

CHICKEN AND MANGO SALAD

FISH TEA

(Serves 4)

*This is a traditional West Indian soup that on cold winter nights, warmed
me up as I am sure it will you, give it a try*

2	Shallots	**Garnish**		
200 g	Tomatoes (ripe, chopped)			
200 g	White fish	1	Tomato (blanched)
2	Garlic cloves	4	Crayfish
1	Scotch bonnet	1	Snapper (filleted)
4	Egg whites			
1 tsp	Coriander			
1 tsp	Basil			
1 ltr.	Fish stock (BASIC 4)			
10	Black peppercorn			
	Salt			

1 Peel shallots and cut in half. Place on fork or skewer and burn over naked flame until well browned or even burnt.
2 Place tomatoes, fish, shallots, garlic, scotch bonnet, egg whites, and herbs into a food processor and blend. Put into a thick bottomed large saucepan.
3 Add cold fish stock and place over a low heat and bring to the boil. Add the peppercorns.
4 Allow to gently simmer for 15 minutes.
5 Pass the tea through a muslin and place into a clean saucepan. Season with salt.

To serve: Place the cooked langoustines, poached fish fillet cut into half and chopped tomatoes into serving dish, and then pour on the hot tea.

- SOUPS AND STARTERS -

FISH TEA

CALYPSO GRILLED PIGEON SALAD

(Serves 4)

2   Plump woodpigeon breasts

Marinade   **Salad**

1   Garlic clove   1 Avocado
1   Orange juice and zest   ¼ Red onion
1   Lemon juice and zest   2 Oranges
½   Scotch bonnet   1 Lemon
1 tsp   Fresh Thyme (chopped)   1 Tomato (skinned)
           Salt and pepper   1 mango
½ tsp   Ground Allspice

Citrus Vinaigrette (BASIC 11)

1   Blend or puree all the marinade ingredients, place the pigeon breast in
     the marinade and leave to stand for anything from 1 – 3 days.
2   Prepare the salad, peel and slice mango and avocado.
3   Blanch the tomato and remove skin, cut in half then slice.
4   Finely slice the onion, segment the orange and lemon into small
     chunks, and arrange on serving plates.
5   Grill the pigeon, 3 minutes each side and then allow to rest for 3-5
     minutes. Slice into 6 and fan out on a plate.
6   Pour over the vinaigrette and serve.

CALYPSO GRILLED PIGEON SALAD

SPICY CRAB & VEGETABLE ROLLS

(Serves 4)

300g	White crab meat (Picked)
1	Red pepper (diced)
1	Green pepper (diced)
1	Yellow pepper (diced)
1	Aubergine
½	Scotch bonnet
2 tbsp	Coriander
200 ml	Sieved tomatoes
	Sugar
1	Small Onion (Diced)
	Filo pastry

1. To prepare the vegetables, dice the pepper and courgettes, slice the aubergine, and place them in milk to cover. Leave to one side. Finely chop the scotch bonnet
2. Sweat the onions for 2 minutes without colour.
3. Add the pepper, drain the aubergines, and sweat for 3 minutes.
4. Add the scotch bonnet and sieved tomatoes, and gently simmer for 15-20 minutes.
5. Season with salt, pepper and sugar.
6. Whilst the mixture is still hot fold in the crab meat and coriander.
7. Egg wash two sheets of filo pastry and cut in half. Lay 2 tbsp of filling 1 cm from the edge of filo, egg wash the top half and roll from the bottom encasing the mix. Fold in the sides
8. Prepare a saucepan of oil for deep frying. When hot deep fry until golden brown. Remove and place on a paper towel to drain.

To serve: with salad leaves and mango mayonnaise (Basic 12)

FISH

DISH

BLAFF

BROWN FISH STEW

JERK LOBSTER BAKED

TUNA JERK STYLE

BAKED FISH YARD STYLE

PAN ROAST TILAPIA served with tomato sauce

SEAFOOD & CALLALOO TART

DOUBLE BUTTERFISH with citrus butter sauce

STEAMED FISH with ginger butter sauce

JERK SALMON

LAYERED PARROT FISH

ROAST DOCTOR FISH

RUNDOWN MACKERAL TART

BLAFF

(Serves 4)

This dish is apparently named from the sound that is made by the fish when it hits the liquid in the pan.

8x120g	Hake Steaks
1	Lime (juiced)
3	Cloves Garlic (pureed)
1	Scotch Bonnet
1 tsp.	Allspice Berries
1 lt.	Court Bouillon (BASIC 8)
2 tsp.	Chopped Parsley
	Thyme
	Salt & pepper

Garnish

1	Tomato (chopped)
½	Cucumber

1 Season and Marinade the fish in lime juice, garlic, scotch bonnet and allspice berries for 40 minutes room temperature.
2 Bring court bouillon to the boil, then add the fish to the cooking liquor. simmer for 8 - 12 minutes or until fish is firm. Add chopped parsley and thyme.
3 Remove fish from cooking liquor and serve with creamed potato and green banana, with compote of vegetables. (see page 119)

To serve: The fish is then topped with diced seasoned tomatoes and diced cucumber, and a little cooking liquor poured around the fish.

BLAFF

BROWN FISH STEW

(Serves 4)

2 Whole	Snapper	2 Whole	Red mullet
1 Whole	Seabream	1 Whole	Tilapia

1   Lime
50g   Flour with 1 tsp of Cayenne pepper added
4   Shallots (finely chopped)
2   Cloves garlic
3 Sprigs   Thyme
500 ml   Fish Stock
2   Carrots (turned or cut into ¾ of an inch)
1   Cho-cho (turned or cut into ¾ of an inch)
400g   Yam (turned or cut into ¾ of an inch)
2   Green Bananas (cut into 1 inch chunks)
12   Okra
3   Tomatoes (chopped)
1 tsp   Chopped parsley
300 ml   Lamb Sauce (BASIC 6)
           Salt & pepper

1   Check all small bones are removed from fish, and cut the fillets into strips, squeeze over with lime juice.
2   Coat the fish in a mix of flour and cayenne pepper and shallow fry, set to one side.
3   Sweat off the shallots, garlic and thyme in a thick bottom pan for 2 minutes.
4   Add the fish stock and lamb sauce and bring to the boil, add all the vegetables and simmer for 10 minutes.
5   Add the fish and simmer for another 10 minutes, then add the chopped tomato and chopped parsley.

To serve: place in a soup bowl and serve with rice and peas. (BASIC 20)

JERK LOBSTER BAKE

(Serves 4)

A similar dish was cooked for me on a rare visit to stay with my father in America were he as lived for the past 30 odd years. He loved fish and seafood but after all his father owned his own boat and was a fisherman in Jamaica. Every Wednesday exotic fresh fish would be delivered to his home, I was sixteen at the time and just getting into cooking, so in the garden, by the pool, orange and lime tree we scaled and gutted fish, most of them I'd never seen before.
He loved shellfish and so do I,

4 x 900g	Lobsters (cooked)
1 tbsp	Olive oil
1 tsp.	Jerk seasoning
100g	Butter
2	Shallots sliced
1	Clove garlic
2 tsp.	Chopped parsley
1	Lime juice
	Salt & pepper

1. Split the lobster in half lengthways straight down the middle discard the intestines, stomach and loosen the flesh from the shell but do not remove.
2. Take the olive oil and blend with the jerk seasoning, lightly coat the lobsters, place on a baking sheet in the oven 200C for 5 minutes
3. Whilst the lobster is cooking prepare the sauce by heating the butter and sweating off the shallots and garlic. Colour to a nutty brown stage, add chopped parsley and lime juice.
4. Place lobster tails onto the plate and pour the butter sauce over lobster.

To Serve: with rice and peas and compote of vegetables. (see page 119)

JERK LOBSTER BAKE

TUNA JERK STYLE

(Serves 4)

Jerk Marinade (BASIC 18)

4x 200g	Tuna steak
25g	Olive oil
200g	Callaloo
2	Green banana ⎤
300g	Yam ⎬ Garnish
1	Cho-cho ⎦
2	Medium carrots
400g	Mashed potato
1lb	Callaloo
	Salt and pepper

Coconut sauce (BASIC 15)

1   Marinade the tuna for 2 hours in the fridge. Take them out ½ hour before cooking.
2   Season the steaks with salt. Place them under the grill for 6 - 10 minutes.

3   To serve: place a bed of callaloo in the centre of the plate followed by the mashed potato on top. Place the grilled tuna along with the boiled vegetables around centre dish and pour over the coconut sauce.

TUNA JERK STYLE

BAKED FISH YARD STYLE

(Serves 4)

4 small	Gilthead Bream		
1 tbsp	Curry powder		
1	Lime juice		
2	Medium onions sliced		
2	Clove garlic	**Butter Sauce**	
4	Tomatoes (chopped)	1	Lemon
50 g	Hard-dough breadcrumbs	1	Orange
1 tbsp	Parsley (chopped)	2	Shallots
	Salt & pepper		

1   Prepare the fish by removing the centre bone. Making sure your keeping the fish together in a butterfly cut. (see photo below)
2   Dust with curry powder, salt, pepper and juice of one lime.
3   Sweat off the onions with the garlic for 5 minutes, and then add tomatoes and breadcrumbs to bind. Taking the fish, place this mixture in the centre of the fish.
4   Place fish on a baking tray, season with a little salt then bake for 15 - 20 minutes. Gas mark 7.

5   To serve: with citrus butter sauce and vegetables.

butterfly cut

PAN ROAST TILAPIA TOMATO SAUCE

(Serves 4)

4	Tilapia (filleted)
1	Lemon (juice)
1	Onion (medium, chopped)
25g	butter
2 tbs	Oil
1	Chilli (chopped fine)
2	Cloves of garlic
50g	White wine vinegar
	Sprig of thyme
400 g	Tomatoes (chopped)
250mls	Sieved tomato
	Sugar (to season)
	Salt & pepper

Ocho Rios cabbage (see page 120)

1. Score the skin on the fillet of fish, then season with lemon, salt and pepper.
2. Sweat the onions in a little oil, adding the chilli and garlic.
3. Add the white wine vinegar and thyme, and reduce by half.
4. Put in the two types of tomatoes then simmer for 15 minutes.
5. Puree and pass into a clean pan adjust consistency and season with a little sugar to taste.
6. Heat a oil and butter in a oven proof frying pan and fry 2 minutes skin side down turn over put in the oven for five minutes.

To serve: Place the fish on the top of Ocho Rios cabbage and rice with sauce served around.

SEAFOOD AND CALLALOO TART

(Serves 4)

1	Fillets Parrot			
1	Tilapia	**Sauce**	
2	Goat fish			
4	Cray fish	3	Shallots
4	Oysters	1 Clove	Garlic
4	Scallops	50 ml	White wine
10 ml	Olive oil	200 ml	Fish stock
2	Shallots (diced)	200 ml	Double cream
200 ml	Fish stock	1 tbsp	Tarragon
50 ml	White wine		
600g	Callaloo		
½ tsp	Nutmeg		
	Salt & pepper		

1   Roll out the puff pastry tarts 10 cm x 7 cm, egg wash then bake at 200C for 15 minutes.
2   To make the sauce heat the oil in the pan, add shallots and sweat for 2 minutes, add the white wine and fish stock, bring to the boil and reduce by half.
3   Add the cream, bring to the boil, and simmer for 15 minutes.
4   Place the 200 ml of fish stock on to boil, add the parrot fish, tilapia and goat fish and cook for 2 minutes, now add the scallops, then after 2 minutes add the crayfish and oysters for the last 2 minutes.
5   Warm the tarts and fry the Callaloo sprinkle with freshly ground nutmeg and season with salt and place in the base of the warmed tart.

To Serve: Take the creamed fish, add the freshly chopped tarragon, place the mix into the tart with the sauce cascading over the sides.

DOUBLE BUTTERFISH
with citrus butter sauce

(Serves 4)

4	Butterfish
3	Oil
25g	Butter

Compote of vegetables (see page 119)

1   Prepare the fish by filleting and de-boning. Cut in half; ensure that all the scales have been removed.
2   Season the fish with salt. In a non stick frying pan fry the fillets for approx 1 ½ minutes, turn over and cook for 30 seconds.

To serve: Assemble the stewed vegetables in the centre of the dish, place the fish on top, and serve with the citrus butter sauce. (BASIC 17)

DOUBLE BUTTERFISH
with citrus butter sauce

SPICY RED SNAPPER

(Serves 4)

4	Red snapper fillets
	Jerk seasoning (BASIC 18)
½	Small Onion
1 clove	Garlic
1 tsp.	Fresh thyme chopped
1 tsp.	Fresh parsley chopped
16	Okra (sliced)
1	Cho-cho (diced)
300 ml	Vegetable stock
1	Green papaya (peeled, de-seeded)

1   Prepare the gutted fish by removing the head and scoring skin, lightly cover in the jerk seasoning leave for 1 hour.
2   Sweat off the onion, garlic, cho-cho, green papaya and okra.
3   Add half the stock and gently cook for 15 minutes, you may need to add more of the stock.
4   Place the fish on a tray and bake for approx 20 minutes.

To serve: Take stewed vegetables add the herbs and lay fish on top. Serve with sauce of your choice.

STEAMED FISH
with ginger butter sauce

(Serves 4)

2	Grey Tilapia
2	Goatfish
2	Snapper
1	Cucumber
2	Escallions
1 tsp	Fresh root ginger (Cut into small dice)
50 ml	White wine
50 ml	Double cream
200g	Butter

1. Scale, gut and fillet fish. (Ask your fish monger and I'm sure he will do this for you).
2. Take the cucumber and peel. Cut into half, and then slice length ways into six. Season the cucumber with salt and citrus vinaigrette (BASIC 11) and place into the steamer and steam.
3. Cut each fillet into two pieces and place in a steamer for 5 minutes.
4. In a sauté pan, sweat of the finely diced escallions, and ginger in a little butter for 2 minutes. (Do not colour).
5. Add the white wine, reduce down then add cream, slowly whisk in the remaining butter. Pass through a sieve.

To serve: Place the cucumber in the centre of the plate and place the fish around the outer plate. Coat with the ginger butter sauce.

JERK SALMON

(Serves 4)

4 x 150gm	Salmon Fillet
	Jerk seasoning (BASIC 18)
25 ml	Olive oil

Sauce

2	Oranges (juice)
1	Lemon (juice)
1	Lime (juice)
1	Mango
3	Tomato
4	Escallion
1	Cucumber
1	Papaya
1 tsp	Tarragon

Side dish

	Callaloo
	Rice and peas (BASIC)

1. Marinade Salmon in jerk seasoning for 2 hours
2. Blanche, skin and chop the tomato then slice the escallion, dice cucumber to the same size as the tomato.
3. Place diced ingredients in a pan cover with stock and then add olive oil
4. Take a non-stick pan place a little oil fry the salmon on each side for 2 ½ minutes
5. Heat pan with the mixed citrus juice, boil for 2 minutes, and remove from heat. Add the diced vegetables and season.

To serve: Serve with callaloo and rice on the side

JERK SALMON

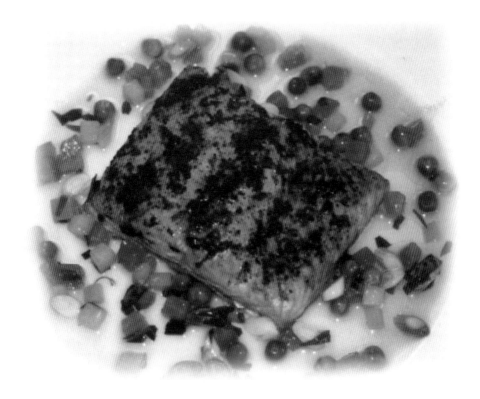

LAYERED PARROT FISH

(Serves 4)

This dish has a great combination of different textures and flavours happening on the plate. This dish I also make with red mullet when parrot fish is not available you can also cook the vegetables and then refresh reheat in a saucepan of salted boiling water

4	Parrot Fish
200 g	New potato (turned)
200 g	Carrots (turned)
1	Plantain (sliced)
500 g	Callaloo
	Oil
15 g	Butter
½ tsp	Nutmeg
	Salt and pepper
	Citrus Sauce (BASIC 11)
8	Filo pastry rectangle (baked)

1. Scale, gut, fillet and bone the Parrot fish and refrigerate.
2. Prepare the potatoes and vegetables and part boil, then refresh.
3. Prepare citrus butter sauce just before you are ready to serve starter.
4. Place pan on the heat, add half oil and butter to fry the fish, a frying pan for cooking the callaloo and a sauce pan for reheating the vegetables and potatoes.
5. Place fish in the frying pan skin side down cook for 4-5 minutes until crispy, then turn over and cook on flesh side for 1 minute.
6. Wilt the callaloo a little oil and butter in a frying pan, season with salt, pepper and nutmeg.

To serve: Place one filo rectangle at the top of the plate, place a layer of callaloo, then fillet of fish then repeat. Take vegetables and arrange at the base of plate and cover with sauce. Brush fish with olive oil.

ROAST DOCTOR FISH

(Serves 4)

4	Doctor Fish (filleted)
50g	Butter

Marinade

1 cm	Fresh Ginger
2 cloves	Garlic
½	Lemon Juice
1 tbsp	Coriander
	Salt and Pepper

Fish sauce (BASIC 5)

1 Take the doctor fish and cut the flesh four times on each fillet.
2 Place fish in marinade for 2 hours.
3 Take a frying pan heat and add the butter then place fillets in skin side down for 3-4 minutes and turn fry for a further 1-2 minutes.

To Serve: With Roasted Vegetables (page 126) and Fish sauce (BASIC 5).

DOCTOR FISH

RUNDOWN MACKEREL TART

(Serves 4)

500 g	Salted Mackerel
2	Shallots
1-2	Garlic
50 ml	White wine
200ml	Fish stock
100 ml	Coconut milk
100 ml	Double Cream
2	Green Banana
½	Scotch bonnet (optional)
4	Puff pastry tart (8-10cm square)

1 Bone and skin the mackerel then soak in cold water overnight.
2 Finely dice the shallots and garlic and place in saucepan, add white wine and fish stock reduce by half .Add the green banana and coconut milk.
3 Simmer for 20 minutes, add the drained salted mackerel and cook for 5 minutes.

To serve: Place puff pastry tart in centre of plate and spoon in the mackerel and cream mix to overflowing, garnish with spring onions and petals of tomato.

RUNDOWN MACKEREL TART

MAIN COURSE

BRAISED OXTAIL with butter beans

ARAWAK PORK

FILLET OF LAMB with coconut sauce

SPICED LAMB

GLAZED DUCK with rum & honey sauce

FILLET OF BEEF with a spiced sauce

JERK PORK FILLET

JERK CHICKEN STUFFED with callaloo & bbq sauce

CORN FED CALYPSO CHICKEN

CREAMY SPICED COCONUT CHICKEN

CURRY SPICY MUTTON

GUINEA FOWL

BEEF STEW

BRAISED OXTAIL with butter bean

(Serves 4)

12 - 16	Cuts of Oxtail
1	Onion
1 tsp.	Allspice
2	Sprigs of Thyme
2	Garlic Cloves
1	Bay Leaf
25 ml	Red Wine Vinegar
25 ml	Oil
2 lt.	Beef Stock (BASIC 6)
150g	Butter Beans (soaked overnight)
1 tsp.	Chilli (optional)
250 ml	Red wine (optional)
4	Tomato (chopped)

1   Marinade oxtails in onion, allspice, thyme, garlic, bay leaf and red wine vinegar for 2 hours.
2   In a frying pan heat the oil and seal the oxtail.
3   When evenly brown remove oxtail from the pan and sweat off the remaining marinade then return the meat to the pan.
4   Add the stock to the pan and bring to the boil, 20 minutes into cooking add the butter beans. Then cook in the oven (gas mark 5, 190C, 375F) for 1 ½ - 2 hours.

To serve: Add chopped tomatoes, parsley and serve with a compote of vegetables (see page 119)

BRAISED OXTAIL with butter bean

ARAWAK PORK

(Serves 4)

1 Rack of Pork

Marinade

2 tbsp	Olive Oil
4	Escallion
2 tsp.	Curry powder
6	Sprig Fresh Thyme
1 tsp.	Chopped parsley
1	Scotch Bonnet
1	Lime Juice
1	Clove of Garlic
1	Bay Leaf

Onion sauce (BASIC 14)

1   Place all the ingredients for the marinade into a blender a puree to a pulp.
2   Smear all over the rack of pork and marinade for 3 hours.
3   Seal the rack in a frying pan until evenly coloured.
4   Roast in the oven for 30 - 40 minutes on gas mark 6, 200C, 400F.
5   Allow to rest for 5 minutes before cutting into portions.

To Serve: With onion gravy on a bed of Ocho Rios cabbage, (see page 120) with rice and peas. (BASIC 20)

FILLET OF LAMB with coconut sauce

(Serves 4)

4	Fillets of Lamb

Marinade:

1	Chilli (Seeded)
1	Coriander
25g	Ginger (finely diced)
1tsp	Cumin Seeds
1tsp	Turmeric
1	Clove of Garlic
50 ml	Olive Oil
2	Shallots (finely sliced)
1	Juice of Lemon
	Coconut Sauce (BASIC 15)

1. Prepare the marinade by blending all the ingredients together.
2. Place the lamb in the marinade and turn occasionally over 2 hours.
3. Take the lamb out of the marinade and set aside.
4. Place marinade into a saucepan and sweat of for 3 minutes, add the coconut sauce and simmer for 30 minutes and then pass through a sieve.
5. Seal lamb fillets in a hot frying pan with a little olive oil.
6. Place into the oven until cooked to your liking, between 8-15 minutes.

To serve: Pour the coconut sauce over the lamb, and garnish serve with mashed potatoes, creamed callaloo and carrots and freshly chopped coriander.

BEEF STEW

(Serves 4)

		Marinade
800 gm	Stewing beef (diced 1inch)	Tomato
1	Onion (medium)	Garlic
	Thyme	Lime
	Beef stock	Thyme
200 ml	Pumpkin puree	Coriander
	Bay leaf	Spices
	Carrots	Olive oil
	Potatoes	
	Coco	evenly turned
	Pumpkin	or diced
	Cho-cho	
	Yam	

1 Marinade the beef for 2 hours.
2 Take the onions and sweat off in a pan, add bay leaf and thyme, cook off gently for 3 minutes.
3 Add the meat to the pan with cold stock and bring to the boil.
4 Allow to gently simmer for approx. 1 ½ - 2 hours.
5 At this stage you can add the vegetables and cook for 10 minutes or until tender.
6 Add the pumpkin puree and cook out for 10 minutes. Season and serve

SPICED LAMB

(Serves 4)

600g	Lamb boneless
1	Scotch bonnet
25g	ground ginger
2	Mixed peppers
4	Spring onion
16	Okra
4 tbsp	Red wine vinegar
	Thyme sauce (BASIC 6)
1spn	Cinnamon
1	Lime juice
1 tsp	Fennel
5 tbsp	Olive oil

1 Slice the lamb into 2 cm strips then put in pre heated pan with Olive Oil then fry for 5 minutes until sealed.
2 Take the ginger escallion, mixed pepper, fennel and fry, adding the vinegar to the Lamb and cook for a further 10 minutes
3 Then add the lime juice for the added flavour of the dish.
4 The meat should be then cooked on a slow heat for 30-40 until tender

To serve: On a bed of rice and peas and vegetables of the season.

GLAZED DUCK
With rum & honey sauce

(Serves 4)

4	Duck breast		
1 tbsp	Honey		**Garnish**
2	Shallots (diced)	1	Plantain
2 tbsp	Honey	4	Pan fried potatoes
25g	Butter	2	Carrots
100 ml	Dark rum		
500ml	Brown chicken sauce (BASIC 2)		
	Salt		

1 Prepare the duck breast by trimming neatly to form a tear drop shape
   For the sauce sweat off shallots in a little oil, add the dark rum and reduce by half.

2 Add the brown chicken sauce, stir in 2 tablespoon honey, and reduce until a nice sauce consistency is achieved.

3 Seal the seasoned duck in the pan, with very little oil then turn skin side up then glaze with honey, place on a tray and put in the oven at 200C for 7 - 10 minute.

4 Peel plantain and fry in the pan used for duck until golden brown.

To Serve: With pan fried potatoes, sliced carrots and plantain

GLAZED DUCK
with rum & honey sauce

FILLET OF BEEF
With a spiced sauce

(Serves 4)

8 200g	Fillet of beef	200g Yam
	Salt	12 Okra
2-3tbs	Coconut oil	1 Aubergines
25g	Butter	

Spiced Sauce

3	Shallots (Sliced)
150 ml	Red wine
1	Scotch bonnet
2 cloves	Garlic
1 tbsp	Olive oil
400 ml	Beef sauce

1. Sweat the shallots in the olive oil, add the finely diced scotch bonnet and garlic.
2. Add the red wine and reduce by half, add the beef sauce and gently simmer for 30 minutes.
3. Heat a frying pan, add the oil and butter. Take the fillets of beef and seal, turn over, and season on both sides.
4. Place them in the oven for 4-8 minutes at 200C, and then allow to rest for 5 minutes in a warm place.
5. Using a 8 cm round cutter, cut out 4 circles from the yam and warm in the oven for 5 minutes, cook off the okra, and then the aubergine in hot oil and butter for 5 minutes. Toss the yam and okra with the aubergines for two minutes and then ready to serve

To serve: Place beef on top of yam, add the sauce then arrange vegetables around the plate.

SPICED FILLET OF BEEF

JERK PORK FILLET

(Serves 4)

900g   Fillet of Pork (prepared weight)
         Jerk Seasoning (BASIC 18)
2Tbsp Jamaican dark rum

         BBQ Sauce (BASIC 9)

1   Marinade the pork in the jerk seasoning for 2 hour.
2   Fry to seal the pork, then bake in oven for 10 – 12 Minutes.
3   Remove from the oven and allow to rest in a warm place.
4   When ready to serve evenly slice the meat and arrange on a warm plate

To Serve: with roasted vegetables and spoon the BBQ sauce over the meat.

JERK CHICKEN
Stuffed with callaloo & BBQ sauce

(Serves 4)

4	Chicken Breast
400g	Callaloo
2	Shallots (sliced)
1	Clove garlic
25g	Butter and oil
Pinch	Nutmeg
Pinch	Salt
4 tbsp	Jerk seasoning (BASIC 18)

BBQ sauce (BASIC 9)

1 Take the chicken breasts and flatten by covering with cling film, then with a large chef's knife gently bat on a chopping board.
2 Fry the shallots without colour, add a little butter and garlic then add the callaloo and wilt. Season with salt and nutmeg then allow to cool.
3 Take the chicken breast skin side down, place on the cling film, add the callaloo mixture in the centre of the breast and roll, put the flattened fillet on the base.
4 Rub the Jerk seasoning over the chicken leave for 1 hour
5 Place oil in a frying pan skin side down sealed and coloured then turn on to the base and place in the oven for 10-12 minutes on gas marked 200 c

To serve: With rice and peas a BBQ sauce.

CORN FED CALYPSO CHICKEN

(Serves 4)

4   Chicken breast

Marinade

2 cloves	Garlic
1	Lemon and grated zest
25 gm	Ginger
1 tsp	Cinnamon
1 tsp	Cumin
1 tsp	Mace
2 tbsp	White wine vinegar
3	Black peppercorns

Sauce

2	Tomatoes (chopped)
100g	Button mushrooms
25 g	Nibbed cashew nuts
1	Mixed peppers (Skinned and diced)
2	Escallion
300 ml	Thyme sauce (BASIC 17)

1. In a pestle and mortar or food processor prepare marinade. Then coat the chicken breast with the marinade for 2 hours. Then remove the chicken from the marinade.
2. For the sauce sweat the escallion, mushrooms, peppers and the marinade for 2 minutes, add the thyme sauce and gently simmer for 15 minute. When ready serve add tomatoes and cashew nuts.
3. Take the chicken and gently fry in oil and butter until golden brown then finish off in the oven for around 8-10 minutes, keep warm.

To serve: With Rice and peas coat the sauce over the chicken.

CORN FED CALYPSO CHICKEN

CREAMY SPICED COCONUT CHICKEN

(Serves 4)

4	Chicken breasts	**Marinade**	
4 tbsp	Coconut oil	3	Cloves garlic
1	Onion (finely chopped)	1 tbsp	Ginger (finely chopped)
300 ml	Chicken stock	1	Scotch bonnet
100 ml	Double cream	2	Cardomon seeds
100 ml	Coconut milk	1 tsp	Ground Cumin
2 tbsp	Coriander (finely chopped)	1 tsp	Ground Cinnamon
1	Juice of lemon	1 tsp	Ground Cloves
		1 tsp	Turmeric
		1 tsp	Paprika
		1 tbsp	Malt vinegar

1. Rinse chicken breast in cold water and vinegar, then drain.
2. Take the garlic, ginger, scotch bonnet and ground spices, and crush together in a pestle and mortar or food processor. Add the chicken and leave to marinade for 2 hours or overnight.
3. Place chicken and marinade into a saucepan and gently seal the meat for 2 – 3 minutes evenly.
4. Add the chicken stock and bring to the boil. Turn down the heat and simmer for 15 minutes.
5. Add the coconut cream and double cream, stir to the boil. Simmer for a further 10 minutes.
6. When ready to serve, check seasoning and add fresh coriander and lemon juice.

To Serve: With Plain Rice.

CURRY SPICY MUTTON

My Uncle George gave me this recipe

1 kg	Boned Mutton

Marinade

1 tsp	Cumin	1 tsp	Fresh ginger
1 tsp	Coriander	½ - 1	Scotch bonnet
1-2 tsp	Turmeric	2 tbsp	Tomato Ketchup
1 tsp	Mace	1	Onion (finely chopped)
1 tsp	Paprika	3	Garlic Cloves
1 tsp	Cinnamon	Pinch	Nutmeg Grated
2 tbsp	Distilled Vinegar		
4 tbsp	Curry powder		
	Coarse black pepper		

700 ml	Lamb stock (BASIC 6)
	Lamb sauce (BASIC 6)
Pinch of	Fresh Thyme, bay leaf, rosemary

1. Dice the lamb 1 ½ inch cubes, place into a stainless steel bowl.
2. Take the marinade ingredients and using a petal and mortar or food processor grind and blend the spices together.
3. Add the marinade to the meat and marinade over night.
4. Seal the meat for 10 minutes in a large saucepan, allowing the marinade to release flavours add curry powder.
5. Add the lamb stock and fresh herbs, and bring to the boil, skim.
6. Simmer for approximately 1 ½ hours, then add the lamb sauce and bring to the boil for 5 minutes. Check seasoning.

To Serve: With Coconut flavoured rice (BASIC 19)

GUINEA FOWL

(Serve 4)

4	Supreme Guinea Fowl
1 tbsp	Coconut Oil
1 tbsp	Butter
Pinch	Salt

Garnish

2	Green Bananas (Boiled)
1	Sweet Potato (Puree)
200 g	Callaloo (fried)

Junja Sauce (BASIC 16)

1 Singe the Guinea Fowl over the gas ring flame to remove stubble.
2 In a stainless steel frying pan add the coconut oil and heat.
3 Place Guinea Fowls skin side down until golden brown and season.
4 Turn over and repeat.
5 Place a knob of butter on each supreme and place in the oven and roast for 10-12 minutes. Baste twice whilst in the oven, take out, and allow to rest.

To Serve: With Sweet Potato (Puree) Boiled Green Bananas with Callaloo in the centre and the Guinea Fowl placed on top, serve sauce around the meat.

GUINEA FOWL

VEGETARIAN

ACKEE TORTE with junja sauce

OKRA PARCELS with sweet pepper sauce

CALLALOO SOUFFLE

YAM & CALLALOO CAKE with

VEGETABLE RICE

LAYERED VEGETABLES

VEGETARIAN CRUMBLE

ACKEE & GREEN BANANA SOUFFLE

CARRIBEAN VEGETABLE PIZZA

ACKEE TORTE
with junja sauce

(Serves 4)

400g	Potatoes (boiled in skins)
100g	Onions
2	Garlic
1tbsn	Oil
3	Tomatoes (blanched and sliced)
200g	Ackee
200g	Puff pastry
10 leaves	Savoy cabbage (blanched)
1	Egg (beaten)
	Thyme
	Salt and pepper

1 Take the boiled cold potatoes and cut them into 4mm slices.
2 Slice the onion and finely chop the garlic, place in a saucepan with a little oil, and gently cook until onions are soft. Allow to cool.
3 Blanch the tomatoes and peel then slice into 4 mm thick strips.
4 Take the Ackee and drain, then rinse in cold water. Add the onions and season with a little salt and pepper.
5 Roll out the pastry to around 3 mm thick. Using a 12 cm pastry cutter cut the pastry into 4 circles (these will be the base) and using a 14 cm pastry cutter cut 4 circles (these will be used for the tops).
6 Take the bottom pastry and place onto baking sheet.
7 Line the inside of a 10 cm wide x 5cm deep (approx.) bowl with cabbage, overlapping. Place a layer of ackee mix then a layer of tomatoes and then finish with a layer of potatoes. Tip the mould upside down onto puff pastry discs, egg wash the sides lightly.
8 Place the top disc on gently. Seal the two discs together using the back of a 10 cm cutter or fingers (be careful not to cut right through the pastry).

9   Glaze with egg wash. Make a small incision in the centre using a knife. You can decorate the top using pastry shapes e.g. diamonds.
10 Bake in a preheated 220C oven for 10 minutes turning down to 200C for an extra 5 – 10 minutes until risen and golden.

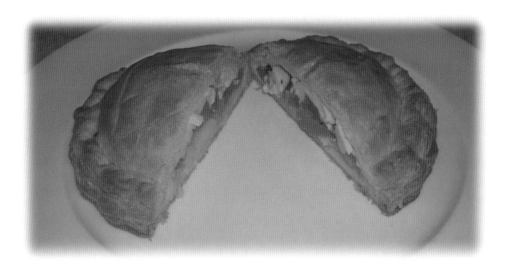

OKRA PARCELS
with sweet pepper sauce

(Serves 4)

1	Onion
1	Cho-cho
2 cloves	Garlic
200g	Sweet potato (diced)
1	Green banana
1 sprig	Thyme
50 ml	Double cream
8 leaves	Filo pastry
1	Egg wash
200g	Okra
100g	skinned green peppers
100ml	Vegetable stock (BASIC 7)
50g	mixed nuts

1   Take a saucepan and gently sweat the onions, cho-cho and garlic for 5 minutes without colour.
2   Add the diced sweet potatoes, green bananas and thyme, then sweat for a further 5 minutes, then add all the other ingredients bring stock to the boil and slowly thicken and reduce down.
3   Add the double cream and continue to cook for 5 minutes, allow to cool.
4   Prepare the filo pastry by brushing with egg wash. Two sheets in thickness.
5   Cut into halve, and then place filling in the centre, fold over the edges then seal. Place the other half in centre of the mix and fold again. Brush with egg wash spread nuts on top and place on baking sheet.
6   Cook in a pre-heated oven, 190C/ 375F gas mark 5 for 15- 20 minutes or golden brown

To Serve: With rice and peas pepper sauce.

OKRA PARCELS
with sweet pepper sauce

CALLALOO SOUFFLE

(Serves 4)

This is a great dish for vegetarians; you've got to try it!

50g	Butter
50g	Flour
400 ml	Milk
100g	Callaloo
5	Eggs (separated)
	Vegetable stock (BASIC 7)
Pinch	Nutmeg
1 Clove	Garlic
1	Cucumber

1   Take the butter and flour and make a roux, add the warm milk gradually. Once all the milk is added cook out gently for 15 minutes.
2   Take the callaloo and cook in butter and a little vegetable stock, place in a blender and puree until smooth.
3   Take the soufflé moulds and coat in butter then repeat place in the fridge.
4   Take the cucumber, peel and cut into thin strips, then line the baking ring.
5   Pass the sauce through a sieve into a bowl, then add egg yolks, beat in well then add the callaloo. Whisk the egg whites with a pinch of salt until stiff, take one third of the whites and mix in to the callaloo mix, add the remainder of the egg whites and fold in with a metal spoon gently until whites evenly distributed.
6   Place mix in the moulds and bake in pre-heated oven 200c for 12-15 minutes.

Serve straight away.

YAM & CALLALOO CAKE
with sauce

(Serves 4)

400g	Yam
25g	Butter
100g	Callaloo
1	Onions
1 tsp	Scotch bonnet
50 ml	Cream
½ tsp	Nutmeg
1	Garlic
100g	Flour
1	Egg
100g	Hard dough breadcrumbs
	Oil (For shallow frying)

1   Peel and roughly chop the yam into dice, place straight into water with a little lemon juice. Boil until tender, for around 15-20 minutes. Drain and lightly dry over a gentle heat. Add the butter and mix in mash.
2   Shred the callaloo and slice the onion, finely chop the scotch bonnet and sweat in a pan 5 minutes. Add the cream, nutmeg and garlic and remove from the heat.
3   Mix all the ingredients together and separate into eight. Shape the cakes and pass through flour, egg and breadcrumbs, do this twice to ensure cakes are well covered.
4   Shallow fry until golden brown.

VEGETABLE RICE

(Serves 4)

200g	Kidney Beans
1	Plantain
2	Green Banana
1	Lemon juiced
1 ½	Pepper (Mixed)
1	Onion
3 Cloves	Garlic
1 tsp	Ginger
½	Scotch bonnet
12-14	Okra
1	Cho-cho
400g	Rice
1 tbsp	Coriander
600 ml	Vegetable Stock (BASIC 7)
2 sprigs	Thyme
200g	Carrot

1 Soak the kidney beans overnight, rinse and place in a saucepan with cold water. Bring to the boil and cook for 40-50 minutes until soft. Save 200ml of the cooking liquor before draining.
2 Prepare the plantain and green banana in triangular chunks 1inch in length.
3 Place in cold water with lemon juice (to prevent discolouring).
4 Dice the mix peppers ¾ inch square. Dice onions, garlic, ginger and scotch bonnet. Cut okra in half and dice cho-cho.
5 Sweat off the onions, garlic, ginger and add the vegetables. Sweat for 2 minutes. Add the rice and kidney beans then gradually add the cooking liquor and vegetable stock. Ladle by ladle until the rice has absorbed the liquid and cooked.

To Serve: Add the chopped herbs and serve.

LAYERED VEGETABLES

(Serves 4)

600g	Callaloo	1	Onions
75 – 100 g	Butter	5 tbsp	Olive oil
2 cloves	Garlic	50 ml	White wine Vinegar
½ tsp	Nutmeg	2	Beef Tomatoes
1	Aubergine	200g	Ackee
50 ml	Vegetable stock	12	Puff Pastry Disc (8 cm)
2	Pepper (red & yellow)		

1   Prepare the callaloo by cooking in a frying pan add 25 g butter and a little water, then add a little garlic and nutmeg.
2   With the aubergine, slice and fry in 25 g butter and 2 tbsp of oil.
3   Burn the pepper skin and evenly slice, take the onions and slice the same thickness as the peppers, place them in a frying pan with a little of olive oil, add the vinegar and season, allow liquid to evaporate.
4   Blanche tomatoes and drain ackee and put to one side.
5   To serve arrange on a large tray all the vegetables add a knob of butter and couple of tablespoons of vegetable stock cover with foil and place in the oven for 8-10 minutes reheat the callaloo in a pan.
6   Take the pastry disc place at the bottom work quickly with on the callaloo, aubergine and peppers put on another layer of puff pastry then place heated tomatoes and ackee on top serve.

To Serve: With Plain Rice.

VEGETARIAN CRUMBLE

(Serves 4)

300g	Gungo peas	**Crumble Mix**	
1 small	Onion		
2	Garlic	40-50 g	Butter
1	Cho-cho	200 g	Hard dough breadcrumbs
1	Plantain	2	Escallion
1	Green banana	1 tsp	Thyme
200g	Bread fruit	1 tsp	Parsley
200g	Tomatoes (pureed)	1 tsp	Coriander
100g	Puff pastry	50 g	Ground Nuts

1. Soak the gungo peas beans overnight. Rinse, and then boil for 30-40 minutes until tender.
2. Dice the onions, and finely chop the garlic.
3. Prepare all the vegetables by cutting into 2 cm cubes.
4. Sweat onions in butter, add the vegetables and gently cook. Mix in the pureed tomatoes, bring to boil then cover with lid and simmer for 5 minutes.
5. Add the gungo peas and garlic and cook for a further 5 minutes.
6. Line the tart with puff pastry and bake blind at 200C for 15-20 minutes.
7. Prepare crumble mix by melting the butter, sweating off the finely diced escallions, and then adding the rest of the ingredients and mix together.
8. Place vegetable mix into tarts and then put crumble mix on top.
9. Bake for 15 minutes at 180C.

To Serve: On a bed of callaloo with Junja sauce (BASIC 16).

ACKEE & GREEN BANANA SOUFFLE

(Serves 4)

200 g	Green banana	Garnish
50 g	Butter	2 green bananas (boiled)
50 ml	Double Cream	2 baby aubergines
50 ml	Milk	100g gungo peas
3	Egg yolks	100g Ackee
½ tsp	Cayenne pepper	50g butter
25 g	Cheese	12 okra
200 g	Ackee	
4	Egg whites	

1 Take the green bananas and boil in its skin for 20 minutes. Once cooked remove skin and puree or mash the green banana and pass through a sieve.
2 Add the butter, cream, milk, egg yolks, cayenne pepper and grated cheese.
3 Take the ackee and beat smooth, add to the mix.
4 Whisk the egg whites with a pinch of salt until stiff. Fold a third of the egg whites into the mix, then gently fold in the remainder. Place into the soufflé moulds and bake in moderate oven 200C / gas 6, for 20 minutes until well risen.
5 Peel and slice bananas slice aubergines heat oil and butter in a frying pan and fry turning for a couple of minutes add ackee season reheat gungo peas in hot water drain and add to vegetables

To Serve: place soufflé in the centre of the plate add onion sauce and arrange vegetables.

ACKEE & GREEN BANANA SOUFFLE

CARIBBEAN VEGETABLE PIZZA

(Serves 4)

<u>Dough</u>

300 ml	Milk
300 ml	Water
500 g	Plain Flour
30 ml	Olive oil
1 tsp	Salt
Pinch	Sugar
15 g	Yeast

<u>Topping</u>

1 tbsp	Oil
50 g	Onion (finely chopped)
100 g	Tomato (sieved)
1 tsp	Thyme
1 tsp	Basil
1	Bay leaf
25 g	Tomato puree
1-2 cloves	Garlic (finely chopped)
50 g	Green Banana (Sliced)
50 g	Cho-cho
100 g	Callaloo
25g	Butter
100 g	Pepper
300 g	Tomatoes (peeled)
100 g	Cheese (grated)
	Salt and pepper

1   Mix together the milk and the water.
2   To make the dough, sieve the flour into a mixing bowl, add the oil, salt and sugar. Mix together.
3   Add the milk and water and incorporate into the flour using one hand. Allow the dough to come together. Do not force the dough.
4   Add the yeast and knead the dough until it comes away from the sides of the bowl clean. Knead into a ball and cover bowl with cling film and leave to rest for 30 minutes or doubled in size.
5   For the sauce, take a sauce pan with a tablespoon of oil and sweat off the diced onions. Add the tomato, herbs, bay leaf and tomato puree. Bring to the boil, and then gently simmer for 15 minutes.

6 Mix in the finely chopped garlic and cook for 5 minutes.
7 Blanch the bananas and cho-cho.
8 Wash the callaloo, and cook quickly in a pan with a knob of melted butter. When cooked, season with salt.
9 Slice tomatoes and peppers.
10 Take your pizza dough and roll out into two even circles, about 7 mm thick. Pierce with a fork.
11 Place the tomato sauce on the pizza base and add the vegetables. Then add the cheese.
12 Bake in oven for 15-20 minutes.

To Serve: With a Mixed Salad.

VEGETABLES

COMPOTE OF CARIBBEAN VEGETABLES

OCHO RIOS CABBAGE

CALLALOO

SWEET POTATOES & ONION

CURRIED OKRA FRIED

GREEN BANANA CHIPS

MIXED VEGETABLES GRATIN

BREADFRUIT CHIPS

CHO-CHO GRATIN

ROAST VEGETABLES

COMPOTE OF CARIBBEAN VEGETABLES

(Serves 4)

200g	Yam (1.5cm diced)
2	Green Banana (1 cm sliced)
½	Lemon (juice)
1	Onion (small diced)
1	Cho-cho (1.5cm diced)
200g	Squash / pumpkin (diced)
200 ml	Tomato sieved
200 ml	Vegetable stock
2 cloves	Garlic (chopped finely)
2 tbsp	Olive Oil
	Salt and pepper

1   Prepare the yam and green banana, place in a bowl with a squeeze of lemon juice.
2   Take the onion and sweat off in a sauce pan with a little oil, add the yam, banana, cho-cho and squash. Cook gently for 2 minutes.
3   Add the tomato and stock and bring it to the boil, turn down to simmer for 20 minutes.
4   Add garlic and check seasoning.

OCHO RIOS CABBAGE

(Serves 4)

450g	Cabbage
225g	Carrot
1 sprig	Fresh Thyme
½	Medium Onion (sliced)

1. Slice the cabbage into thin strips, cut the carrots in half lengthways and slice around 3 mm thick
2. Melt the butter in a pan, add the onion and thyme and sweat off for 2 minutes, add the carrots and cabbage, cook for 2 minutes.
3. Add the vegetable stock then steam for 12-15 minutes. Season.

CURRIED OKRA FRIED

(Serves 4)

16	Okra fingers
75g	Flour
1tbsp	Curry powder
	Salt and pepper

1. Prepare a pan with oil for deep frying the okra.
2. Trim the okra and coat in the flour and curry mix.
3. Then fry until lightly crisped and golden, about 2-3 minutes.

CALLALOO

(Serves 4)

600g	Callaloo
½ tsp	Nutmeg
25g	Butter
25-50ml	Water
	Salt

1. Pick and wash the callaloo.
2. Take a shallow sauce pan, melt the butter, add the water and callaloo leaves.
3. Season with nutmeg and salt. Drain and serve as required.

If fresh callaloo is not available, spinach can be substituted.

SWEET POTATOES & ONION

(Serves 4)

400g	Sweet potatoes
100g	Onions (sliced)
25g	Butter
25g	Oil
1 tsp	Coriander (chopped)
	Salt

1. Boil the potatoes in their skin until almost cooked.
2. Allow to cool, and then peel and slice.
3. Take a pan, put onto the heat place in the oil and butter.
4. Lightly fry the onions, add the potatoes, and toss in the pan until golden.
5. Season with salt and sprinkle on coriander.

GREEN BANANA CHIPS

(Serves 4)

2	Green bananas
	Oil (for deep frying)
	Salt

1. Prepare the oil to deep fry the bananas.
2. With a sharp knife score down the natural lines of the banana and peel by hand.
3. Slice the banana 1-2 mm thin, sprinkle separately into hot oil pan.
4. Once golden brown, place on kitchen paper.
5. Lightly season with salt

MIXED VEGETABLES GRATIN

(Serves 4)

50 ml	Coconut milk
2	Green bananas (sliced)
200g	Breadfruit (diced)
200g	Yam (diced)
1 sprig	Thyme
50g	Cheese (grated)

1 Cook the vegetables in a pan of boiling water, enough to cover the vegetable. Cook for 15 minutes
2 Add the thyme and coconut cream. Cook for 10 minutes.
3 Place in a vegetable serving dish.
4 Sprinkle the cheese over the top and glaze under the grill. Sprinkle with chopped herbs.

BREADFRUIT CHIPS

(Serves 4)

300g   Breadfruit
        Oil (deep frying)

1   Peel the breadfruit
2   Trim away the core, and slice into 4cm by 1cm chips.
3   Place them straight into lemon water.
4   Drain from the water.
5   Fry the breadfruit in hot oil.
6   Drain on to kitchen towel and serve.

CHO-CHO GRATIN

(Serves 4)

3	Cho-cho
1	Onion
250 ml	Double cream
250 ml	Milk
1 clove	Garlic (pureed)
50g	Cheese
1 tsp	Chopped Parsley

1. Peel the cho-cho and cut into half, and de-seed.
2. Slice cho-cho and onions, sweat of in a frying pan.
3. Add the cream, milk and garlic, and season.
4. Place in an ovenproof dish and cover with grated cheese.
5. Bake in the oven at 200C for 20 minutes, until golden brown, and sprinkle with chopped parsley.

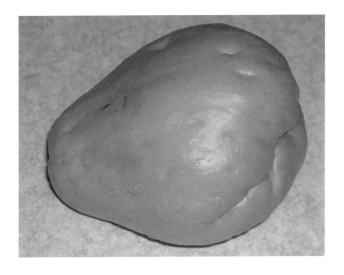

ROAST VEGETABLES

(Serves 4)

1	Cho-cho
200g	Yellow or white yam
200g	Coco
	Whole Garlic
200g	Carrots
200g	Onions
1 tsp	Brown Sugar
50 ml	Olive oil
	Fresh Thyme

1   In an oven proof pan add the oil and slightly brown the vegetables.
2   Season with salt and sprinkle with sugar.
3   Place in the oven, turning throughout the cooking.
4   Cook for 20 minutes at 200C

DESSERTS

RUM & RAISIN CHEESECAKE

RUM TRIFLE

PINEAPPLE & BANANA CRUMBLE

BLUE MOUNTAIN COFFEE CRYSTAL MOUSSE

STEAMED BANANA PUDDING

PINEAPPLE TART

PUMPKIN PIE

JAMAICAN GINGER PUDDING

BREAD PUDDING

MANGO & PAWPAW TOWER

MIXED TROPICAL FRUIT TART

TRIPLE CHOCOLATE DELIGHT

JAMACIAN ORANGE CREAMED ICE

RUM & RAISIN CHEESECAKE

(Serves 4-8)

I don't really like cream cheese, so I adapted this recipe using close to half the usual amount. This gives the cheesecake a light creamy texture. With the raisins and the rum, this is a dessert I'm sure those of you who don't normally like cheesecake will enjoy

50 g	Butter
250 g	Digestive Biscuits
3 leaves	Gelatine
200 g	Cream Cheese
150 g	Caster Sugar
75 g	Raisin
75 ml	Rum
250 ml	Cream (whipped)
2 tbsp	Apricot Jam

1. Crush the digestive biscuits to breadcrumbs in consistency.
2. Melt the butter and add to the biscuit crumb, mix together.
3. Line the tin with the Biscuit mix and refrigerate for 10-15 minutes.
4. Soak the gelatine in cold water for 15 minutes to soften.
5. Beat together the sugar and cream cheese, then take the raisins and rum, place in a sauce pan and bring to the boil, add the gelatine and dissolve.
6. Stir this into the cheese mixture then fold in the whipped cream.
7. Place the mixture into the mould with the cheesecake base.
8. Ensure that all mix is press down, and smooth on the top.
9. Glaze with Apricot jam, a few raisins, and chocolate shavings.

RUM TRIFLE

(Serves 4)

	Trifle Sponge (BASIC 24)
	Pastry Cream (BASIC 23)
4 tbsp	Black Berry Jam
100 ml	Stock Syrup
4 tbsp	Dark Rum
4 tbsp	Over proof white rum/White rum
4 tbsp	Sherry
150 ml	Double or Whipped Cream
2 tbsp	Icing Sugar

Garnish

½	Mango
25 g	Toasted Coconut
½	Pineapple chunks (tinned or fresh)

1   Take the trifle sponge and spread them with the jam.
2   The press the sponges into the bowl.
3   Boil the stock syrup, both rums and sherry for 2 minutes and soak the sponges with the syrup mix.
4   Take the warm pastry cream and add as the next layer. Once cooled add the whipped cream flavoured with icing sugar to taste.

Garnish: the Top of the trifle with mango, pineapple and toasted coconut or chocolate. (As in picture)

RUM TRIFLE

PINEAPPLE & BANANA CRUMBLE

(Serves 4-6)

A crumble to me is, that any time, any where type of dish.

	Sweet pastry (BASIC 22)
150g	Flour
50-75g	Demerara Sugar
150g	Butter
25g	Coconut
25g	Oats
2	Apples (peeled, cored & sliced)
1 small	Pineapple (peeled, cored and diced)
1	Banana (sliced)
1 tsp	Cinnamon
1 tsp	Mixed Spice
½	Lemon Juice

1 Line 6 pastry cases with sweet pastry,
2 For the crumble, take the flour, sugar and mix together.
3 Add the coconut, oats, and butter and then mix together. Everything should be loosely combined to resemble breadcrumbs.
4 Chop the apple, pineapple and banana then mix with the spice and lemon juice. A little sugar can be added to sweeten.
5 Place filling into the tart moulds and then cover with crumble mix.
6 Bake in a preheated oven for approximately 20-25 minutes at 200C.

To Serve: With fresh cream or vanilla ice cream.

PINEAPPLE & BANANA CRUMBLE

BLUE MOUNTAIN COFFEE CRYSTAL MOUSSE

(Serves 8)

250ml	Milk
100 g	Sugar
2 tbsp	Blue Mountain Coffee
4	Egg yolks
3 Leaves	Gelatine (1 tbsp powdered gelatine)
1 tbsp	Kuala
400ml	Cream (Whipped)
3 tbsp	Rum
100 ml	Stock syrup (BASIC 25)
2	Circles of Coffee Sponge (genoise on swiss roll tray)

Crystal Jelly

100ml	Stock syrup
½ tsp	Coffee
2 Leaves	Gelatine (1 tsp powdered gelatine)

1   Bring the milk to the boil with half sugar and coffee, whisk the remaining sugar and egg yolk in a stainless steel bowl.
2   Take the milk and pour onto whisked egg yolk, then return to saucepan, cook the mix until it coats the back of the spoon.
3   Add the soaked gelatine (powdered gelatine) and coffee liquor, then cool on a bed of crushed ice. Add the whipped cream to the mixture.
4   Take the sponge and place in a cake ring; soak with rum and stock syrup.
5   Spoon in half of the mix, then add the other sponge, soak and add the remainder of coffee mousse.
6   Set in fridge for 3 hours or more.
7   Prepare jelly by heating up the stock syrup and coffee, add the gelatine and place in the fridge to just setup

8   Once ready cut up to resemble crystals and spread over the top of mousse
     and place in fridge until ready to serve.

To Serve: With a orange sauce and segments. (BASIC 26)

STEAMED BANANA PUDDING

(Serves 4)

With this pudding, diets and healthy eating will have to be put on hold.

100 g	Brown Sugar
100 g	Butter
2	Eggs
150 g	Flour
10 g	Baking Powder
2	Banana
1 tsp	Cinnamon
1 tsp	Mixed Spice

1. Cream the sugar and butter together.
2. Add the eggs, flour and baking powder gradually.
3. Mix in the bananas, cinnamon and mixed spice.
4. Place the mixture into individual well greased dariole moulds and cover the tops with grease proof paper.
5. Steam for 40 - 50 minutes.
6. Remove from moulds and reheat when required.

To Serve: With Butterscotch Sauce lightly whipped cinnamon cream and fresh sliced bananas. (BASIC 27)

STEAMED BANANA PUDDING

PINEAPPLE TART

(Serves 4)

Topping

125 g	Butter
125 g	Sugar
3	Eggs
90 g	Plain Flour
50 g	Cornmeal
1 tbsp	Baking Powder
50 g	Ground Almonds
1	Lemon & Zest
50g	Mixed Nuts

Filling

1 whole	Pineapple Diced
1 tsp	Mixed Spice
3 tbsp	Icing Sugar

Cinnamon Pastry

200 g	Flour
1 tbsp	Cinnamon
50 g	Sugar
	Pinch Salt
100 g	Butter
1	Egg
25 ml	Cold water

1. Prepare the pastry by sieving the flour and cinnamon. Add sugar and salt, and mix in.
2. Add the butter and rub into a breadcrumb texture. Add the egg and water and lightly mix until comes together. Wrap in cling film and place in fridge.
3. Take the pineapple and top and tail, peel with a sharp knife. Cut deep enough to miss the brown circles under the skin. Cut into quarters and remove the core. Cut each quarter into 3-4 strips, then cut into 1 cm squares.
4. In a saucepan add the pineapple (saving a few squares for garnish), add the mixed spice and icing sugar, and cook until pineapple in caramelised. Allow to cool.
5. Taking the butter, sugar, cream together. Add the egg, sieved flour, cornmeal, baking powder and ground almonds, mix together and add the lemon and zest.
6. Roll out the pastry and line a 7 inch tart mould, place the pineapple onto the base, them cover with creamed mix. Sprinkle nuts on top and bake in oven gas 200C for 30-40 minutes.

To Serve: with Malibu flavoured cream, vanilla sauce and dust with icing sugar.

PUMPKIN PIE

(Serves 8-10)

Sweet Pastry (BASIC 22)

4	Eggs
250 ml	Double cream
125 ml	Milk
125 ml	Maple syrup
50 g	Sugar
200 g	Pumpkin puree
2 tbsp	Flour
½ tsp	Nutmeg
½ tsp	Ground Ginger
1 tsp	Cinnamon

1   Roll out pastry and line a 10 inch pie tin.
2   In a bowl mix together eggs, cream and milk.
3   Add the maple syrup, sugar and pumpkin puree.
4   Season with the nutmeg, ground ginger and cinnamon.
5   Carefully pour the mixture into the pie tin and place in oven.
    160 C / Gas 5 for approx. 30 – 40 minutes or until set.

JAMAICAN GINGER PUDDING

(Serves 4)

150 g	SR Flour
1 tsp	Mixed Spice
3 tsp	Ginger
1 tsp	Bicarbonate of soda
75 g	Soft dark brown sugar
100 g	Golden syrup
50 g	Treacle
75 g	Butter
100 ml	Milk
2	Eggs

1 Sieve flour, mixed spice, ginger and bicarbonate of soda into a mixing bowl.
2 Place sugar, golden syrup, treacle and butter into a saucepan and heat until melted together. Remove from the heat.
3 Add the milk to the melted mix and mix in well
4 Quickly mix in the beaten eggs.
5 Pour the mix into the flour mix and fold in well.
6 Prepare 8 dariole moulds by lightly buttering.
7 Fill the moulds just over half and place on a baking tray.
8 Place the baking tray into a medium oven 180C for 25 minutes.

BREAD PUDDING

(Serves 4)

While we were growing up, my mum would make this. I enjoyed it then and I still do. I've added a few extras of my own. See what you think.

75 g	Brown sugar
4	Eggs
200 ml	Milk
100 ml	Double Cream
½ tsp	Nutmeg
1 tsp	Cinnamon
½ tsp	Almond essence
½ tsp	Vanilla essence
1 tsp	Mixed spice
10	Slices hard dough bread
50 g	Raisins
50 g	Sultanas
200 ml	Coconut milk
50 g	Golden caster sugar

1 Whisk the sugar and eggs together, and then add the milk and cream. Pass through a sieve or conical strainer.
2 Mix in the spice and essence.
3 Take the bread and put in a blender and make breadcrumbs
4 Put the breadcrumbs into a baking dish and add the egg mix, allow it to soak in for 10 minutes. Add the raisins, sultanas and coconut milk and gently mix in.
5 Place into a bath of water and bake in the oven at 180C for 30-40 minutes.

To serve: sprinkle liberally with golden caster sugar and glaze under a grill or with a blow torch. Serve with cinnamon sauce and caramelised apple. (sliced apples coated with icing sugar and toss in a pan).

MANGO & PAWPAW TOWER

(Serves 4)

1	Mango
1	Pawpaw
250 ml	Cream
100g	Pastry Cream (BASIC 23)
12	Puff pastry discs
	Liquor to taste

1. Roll the puff pastry and using a 3 inch round cutter cut out 12 discs, bake by placing on a baking tray and placing another baking tray on top of the pastry to keep them flat.
2. Cook for 10 Minutes at gas 200C. Allow them to cool.
3. Peel and de-seed the pawpaw and mango and dice small.
4. Whisk the cream until stiff and fold it into the pastry cream, then the flavour with liquor.
5. Place into a piping bag and neatly pipe around the sides of 4 pastry discs; add paw-paw and mango to the centre. Add the next pastry disc on top and add more cream and fruit.
6. Add the final disc and dust with icing sugar.
7. Take a steel rod and place on a naked flame until it is very hot. Now being very careful, scorch diamonds on top.

To Serve: With fruit sauce and/or custard sauce (BASIC 26 or 28).

MANGO & PAWPAW TOWER

MIXED TROPICAL FRUIT TART

(Serves 4)

This tart is best made well in advance. The tart can be filled with any fruits of your choice. The apricot jam is a glaze to preserve the fruit.

200 g	Puff pastry	**Pastry cream**	
100 ml	Whipped cream	1	Egg
½	Mango	2	Yolks
1	Papaya	50 g	Caster Sugar
½	Pineapple	250 ml	Milk
2	Passion Fruit	1 tbsp	Flour
1	Banana	1 Leaf	Gelatine
	Apricot glaze		

1. Roll out the puff pastry to approx. 6mm in thickness. Using a 4inch fluted cutter cut out four rounds. Then using a cutter ½ inch smaller, lightly scour the centre of each round. (Avoid cutting all the way through). Egg wash and rest for 30 minutes in the fridge. Then bake at 200C for 15-20 minutes.
2. Place the tarts on a cooling rack once cooked.
3. Prepare the fruit. Cut the mango along the stone and slice into 8 thick slices. Top and tail the pineapple, peel, cutting deep enough to miss the brown circles under the skin. Remove the core and slice. Peel the papaya and cut in half. Remove all the seeds and slice. Cut the passion fruit in half and remove the seed and flesh. Peel the bananas last, slice into rounds.
4. Beat out the pastry cream; add the liquor before folding in the whipped cream.
5. Place the cream mix into the tarts and set up in the fridge for 1-2 hours.

6   Remove tarts from the fridge and arrange the fruit on top of the cream, then glaze with apricot jam. Return to fridge until an hour before serving.

To serve: Best eaten at room temperature. It can be eaten with a fruit couli or plain.

TRIPLE CHOCOLATE DELIGHT

(Serves 4)

This is one of Tracey's favourite dishes. It was her pregnancy dessert, due to it not having any eggs in it. I removed these from the original recipe.

200g	Milk Chocolate
200 ml	Double Cream
1 leaf	Gelatine
200g	White chocolate
150 ml	Double Cream
1 ½ leaves	Gelatine
200g	Plain chocolate
200 ml	Double cream

Sponge

4	Eggs
100g	Sugar
100g	Flour
25g	Cocoa powder

1 Prepare the sponge by whisking the eggs and sugar to a ribbon stage. Sieved flour and cocoa powder together. Add to the eggs and fold in with a large spoon.
2 Working quickly, spread the sponge mix onto a tray, as if making a swiss roll. Bake for 6-8 minutes at 180C.
3 Once sponge is cool, cut out four bases to the size of the mould being used.
4 Place the sponges into the moulds.
5 Take the white chocolate and cut into small pieces. Place into a stainless steel bowl and place over a pan of gently boiling water and melt. Once melted, dissolve 1 leaf of gelatine in a couple of tablespoons of heated rum or water
6 Whisk the cream and add to the melted chocolate, beat together well.

7   Half fill the moulds with the white chocolate mix.

8   Do the same with the milk chocolate, melt chocolate, add gelatine, add whisked cream and fill the moulds to the top.

9   Place the filled mould in the fridge whilst you prepare the dark chocolate.

10   To do this, chop up the dark chocolate into really small bits with a sharp knife, and place in a large bowl.

11   In a saucepan add the double cream and gently bring to the boil.

12   Once cream starts to boil, add it straight away to the chopped chocolate and mix until all the chocolate has melted.

13   Whilst the chocolate mix is cooling to a coating consistency, remove the mousses from the mould. Place them on a cooling tray over a metal tray.

14   Using a ladle, pour the chocolate mix over the mousse, you can do this a few times for a thicker coating. Then return to fridge until needed.

To serve: Sprinkle with a little ground peanut brittle in a fruit couli.

JAMAICAN ORANGE CREAMED ICE

(Serves 4)

For texture, I like to grind nut brittle and then add it to the mix with cream.

5	Egg yolks
75g	Sugar
25 ml	Water
125 ml	Orange juice
2 tbsp	Orange Liquor
250 ml	Double cream
1 tsp	Cinnamon

Orange sauce

200 ml	Orange juice
50g Sugar	
1 tsp	Corn flour

1. Add the sugar to water and bring to the boil, removing all impurities with a very clean pastry brush as they come to the surface. Cook to a temperature of 125C
2. Separate the egg yolks and lightly whisk.
3. Slowly pour the cooked sugar onto the egg yolks, and then strain the mixture through a sieve.
4. Add the cinnamon, and whisk the egg mixture until it becomes thicker and cooled to a ribbon stage.
5. Whisk the cream, add the juice and liquor to the egg mixture, and then fold in the cream lightly and evenly.
6. Set in a mould
7. For the sauce bring the orange juice to the boil, dissolve corn flour into lemon juice, and add to the hot orange juice.
8. Cook out for 3-5 minutes and leave to cool.

To Serve: with orange sauce and segmented oranges and mint leaves to decorate.

BASICS

WHITE CHICKEN STOCK

BROWN CHICKEN STOCK

CHICKEN SAUCE

FISH STOCK

FISH SAUCE

LAMB STOCK

VEGETABLE STOCK

COURT BOUILLON

BARBEQUE SAUCE

SPICY TOMATO SAUCE

CITRUS VINEGARETTE

MANGO MAYONAISE

RED PEPPER SAUCE

ONION SAUCE

COCONUT SAUCE

JUNJA SAUCE

THYME SAUCE

JERK SEASONING

COCONUT RICE

RICE & PEAS

SAVOURY PASTRY

SWEET PASTRY

PASTRY CREAM

TRIFLE SPONGE

STOCK SYRUP

FRESH FRUIT SAUCE

BUTTER SCOTCH SAUCE

CUSTARD

YOGHURT SAUCE

PEELED TOMATOES

WHITE CHICKEN STOCK
(Basic 1)

(Serves 4)

2	Carrots (roughly chopped)
2	Sticks of Celery (chopped)
1	Leek (Optional)
1	Onion (chopped)
1	Bouquet Garni
3 lb	Chicken Bones
2.5 lt	Water

1 Place all ingredients in to a large pan and bring to boil, then turn down the heat and simmer for approximately 1 ½ -2 hours.
2 Skim throughout cooking.
3 Pass the stock through a fine sieve.

BROWN CHICKEN STOCK
(basic 2)

Note: as for White Chicken Stock, just brown the chicken bones by roasting in oven or sauté on the stove.

CHICKEN SAUCE
(Basic 3)

2	Chicken Stock Brown
1	Onion (Diced Small)
1	Carrot (Finely Chopped)
1	Celery (Sliced)
2 tbsp	Oil
100 ml	White Wine
2 Cloves	Crushed Garlic
Pinch	Rosemary and Thyme
100 ml	Sieved Tomato

1. Take the onion, carrot and celery and fry in the sauce pan with oil, to colour for 2 minutes.
2. Add the white wine, crushed garlic, herbs and tomato and cook for 3 minutes then add the stock and reduce down to half.

FISH STOCK
(Basic 4)

1 kg	Fish bones
1	Onion
1	Carrot
1	Leek
	Bouquet Garni
1 lt	Water

1. Wash the bones and chop into smaller pieces.
2. Place into a large pan along with all the other ingredients.
3. Put to boil, and then simmer for 20 minutes.
4. Skim throughout cooking
5. When finished cooking, pass through a fine sieve.

FISH SAUCE
(Basic 5)

This sauce can be made the day before and kept refrigerated and can be used for a variety of fish dishes with the addition of flavours.

1 tbsp	Butter
2	Shallots
2 cloves	Garlic
100 ml	White wine or dry vermouth
300 ml	Fish stock
250 ml	Double cream
1 tsp	Fresh Herbs (chopped)

1 Melt butter in a saucepan, add shallots, garlic and sweat without colour for 3 minutes.
2 Add the white wine and fish stock, and reduce by just under half.
3 Pour in the cream and stir to the boil. Turn down the heat and gently simmer for approximately 15 minutes, season, add fresh herbs when ready to serve.

LAMB STOCK & SAUCE
(Basic 6)

LAMB STOCK

1 kg	Lamb bones
2	Carrots
2	Onions
1	Leek
2	Celery Sticks
1 tbsp	Tomato Puree
1	Bouguet Garni
3 lt	Water
	Parsley Stalks

1. Roughly chop all vegetable.
2. Brown the bones and vegetable, either by sauté on top of stove, or in a roasting tray in the oven.
3. Once bones and vegetables are browned, place in large heavy saucepan; add tomato puree, bouquet garni and cold water.
4. Bring to the boil and then simmer for 2 ½ - 3 hours, topping up with water through the cooking process and skimming through out.
5. Once cooking has finished, Drain by passing through fine sieve.

LAMB SAUCE

1	Carrot
4	Shallots
4	garlic cloves
200 ml	Red wine
100 ml	Port

1 Take the Lamb stock.
2 Finely chop the carrot, shallots and garlic.
3 Add these to the stained basic lamb stock and bring to the boil.
4 Add red wine and port, and then reduce by a third.

VEGETABLE STOCK
(Basic 7)

2	Onions
1	Leek
2	Carrots
1	Celery stick
½ lb	Pumpkin
1	Cho-cho
4	Garlic clove
1	Water
1	Bouquet Garni

1   Roughly chop all ingredients.
2   Place in large heavy bottom saucepan and add water and Bouquet garni.
3   Bring to the boil, then reduce heat and simmer for 20 minutes.
4   Skim while cooking, then strain through fine sieve.

COURT BOUILLON
(Basic 8)

1	Onion
1	Leek
1	Celery stick
1	Carrot
2	Garlic
1	Lemon
1 ½ lt	Water
200 ml	Dry white wine
6	Pepper Corn
	Bouquet Garni

1   Chop all vegetables and sweat off in heavy bottomed sauce pan.
2   Add water, wine, pepper corns, lemon juice and Bouquet garni.
3   Bring to the boil, then reduce heat and simmer for 20 minutes.
4   Skim while cooking, then strain through fine sieve.

BARBEQUE SAUCE
(Basic 9)

This sauce can be made well in advance and just reheat. It goes well with most of the jerk flavoured dishes

100 ml	Pineapple / orange juice
100 ml	Red wine
25 ml	White wine vinegar
1	Shallot (chopped)
25g	Brown sugar
1 tsp	Fresh Ginger
2 cloves	Garlic
100 ml	Lamb sauce
100 ml	Tomatoes (sieved)
2 tbsp	Honey

1 Take the fruit juice, red wine, white wine vinegar, shallot, sugar, ginger and garlic and put in a pan and bring to the boil.
2 Add the lamb sauce, stir in the tomatoes and honey. Simmer for 15 minutes.
3 Pass through a sieve. Reheat and season, then it is ready to use

SPICY TOMATO SAUCE
(Basic 10)

1 tbsp	Oil
2	Shallots (sliced)
½ -1	Scotch Bonnet
50 ml	Wine vinegar
100 ml	White wine
500 g	Tomatoes Chopped

1   Sweat the shallots and scotch bonnet for 3 minutes without colour.
2   Add the wine and vinegar, and bring to the boil, add the tomatoes and cover with a lid and gently cook, stirring occasionally for 20 minutes.
3   Place mixture into a blender and then pass through a sieve.
4   Check seasoning; adjust with salt, pepper and sugar. If sauce is slightly thick add a little stock.

CITRUS VINIGARETTE
(Basic11)

25 ml	White wine vinegar
2 tsp	Lemon juice
150 ml	Olive oil

1 Place all the ingredients into a bowl and whisk all together.
2 If serving with meat, add 50 ml hazelnut or walnut oil and reduce the amount of olive oil.

MANGO MAYONNAISE
(Basic 12)

100g	Mango
150g	Mayonnaise
100 ml	Chicken stock or vegetable stock
1 tbsp	Tarragon / coriander

1 Puree mango and add to the mayonnaise.
2 Correct consistency by adding a little stock. To finish add herbs.

Mayonnaise

2	Egg yolks
1 tsp	Mustard
1 tsp	White wine vinegar
250 ml	Vegetable oil
	Salt and white pepper

1 Whisk the egg yolks, mustard and vinegar in a bowl.
2 Then in a slow gradual stream, pour the oil into the eggs whilst still whisking all the time.
3 Carry on whisking until all the oil has been added.

RED PEPPER SAUCE
(Basic 13)

3	Red peppers (sliced)
1	Red Onion (sliced)
4 cloves	Garlic (sliced)
200 ml	Sieved tomatoes
200 ml	White wine
200 ml	Vegetable stock
3 tbsp	Olive oil
25 ml	Red wine vinegar
	Seasoning salt and sugar

1. Heat the oil into a frying pan, gently fry without colour, add the peppers and garlic and fry for a few minutes, add the white wine and vinegar and simmer for 2 minutes. .
2. Add the vegetable stock and tomatoes and simmer for approx. 15 minutes.
3. Place into a blender and then pass through a fine sieve, check seasoning, adjust with salt and a little sugar.

ONION SAUCE
(Basic14)

1 tsp	Olive oil
3	Medium Onions (chopped)
1 tsp	Thyme (chopped)
1 tsp	Parsley (chopped)
500 ml	Lamb sauce (BASIC 6)

1. Heat the oil in a saucepan, add the onions, and fry over a steady heat until brown.
2. Add the herbs and lamb sauce, and gently simmer for 20 minutes.

COCONUT SAUCE
(Basic15)

200 ml	Lamb sauce / fish sauce
100 ml	Coconut milk
100 ml	Double cream
1 tbsp	Fresh Coriander
	Salt and Pepper

1. Place the lamb sauce onto the boil with the coconut cream.
2. Simmer for 20 minutes, then seasons.
3. Add the herbs when ready to serve.

JUNJA SAUCE
(Basic 16)

25g	Butter
3	Shallots (sliced)
2 cloves	Garlic (pureed)
75g	Oyster mushrooms
75g	mushrooms (sliced)
150 ml	Dry vermouth
300 ml	Vegetable stock (BASIC 7)
300 ml	Double cream

1 Melt the butter in a saucepan, add the shallots and garlic and gently sweat until soft.
2 Add mushrooms and cook for 2 minutes, turn up the heat slightly.
3 Add the vermouth and reduce by half.
4 Then add the stock and reduce this by half.
5 Mix in the cream and bring to the boil, simmer for 20 minutes.

This sauce can be made in advance and put in the fridge once reheated then check for seasoning.

THYME SAUCE
(Basic 17)

25 g	Butter
2	Shallot (finely chopped)
1 Sprig	Thyme
500 ml	Chicken Sauce
2	Skinned, seeded and chopped Tomatoes

1. Melt butter in pan and sweat shallots until soft, then add the thyme and chicken sauce and bring to the heat and simmer for 30 minutes.
2. Pass through a sieve.
3. When ready to serve check for seasoning and add the tomatoes.

JERK SEASONING
(Basic 18)

	All Spice
4	Escallion (Chopped)
1 tsp	Salt
2-4	Scotch Bonnet (Chopped)
2 Clove	Garlic
1 Sprig	Fresh Thyme
2 cm	Fresh Ginger (Sliced and Washed)
3	Lime Juice
2 tbsp	Dark Rum
4 ¼ tsp	Nutmeg
50 ml	Oil
1 tsp	Ground Mace
1 tsp	Ground Cinnamon
1 tbsp	Malt Vinegar

1. Finely crush allspice in the pesal and morsal or food processor.
2. Add the escallion, salt, ginger, scotch bonnet, garlic and fresh thyme to all the dry ingredients. Blend together to a paste texture then add all liquid ingredients.
3. Store in an air tight container which will retain the moisture when ready to use.

COCONUT RICE
(Basic19)

400 g	Basmati Rice
Pinch	Salt
500 ml	Cold Water
200 ml	Coconut Milk
1 tbsp	Butter
1 tbsp	Fresh Coriander

1. Rinse the rice until the water is clear and place the rice into a pan, add the salt, water and coconut milk stir and bring to boil.
2. When the rice has boiled put on the lid and turn to the lowest heat, this should take 15-20 minutes.

To Serve: With fresh Coriander

CORIANDER

RICE AND PEAS
(Basic 20)

(Serves 4)

This dish can be made with a variety of beans and peas. Rice is something we had to eat on a regular basis when I was younger, mainly because my mother enjoyed it and you know as well has I do that too much of the same thing, so I would just say rice, rice everyday rice. Due to my mother's excellent culinary skills I can honesty say no one cooked rice as good, but I keep trying.

100 g	Kidney Beans (Soaked Overnight)
2 Sprigs	Fresh Thyme
2	Shallots
400 g	Brown Rice
50 g	Coconut Cream
1 tbspn	Butter
1 tsp	Salt

1. Rinse the soaked kidney beans, then place in a large quantity of cold water. Bring to the boil and add the thyme and shallots, and simmer for approximately 1 hour. To check beans are cooked gently squeeze and the beans should be soft to the touch.
2. The water from the beans should have a reddish tint. Add the rice, coconut cream and more water if need, this amount should be around 2 cm above the rice to achieve the right texture.
3. Bring to the boil and then add the butter and turn down to the lowest setting, place the lid on the pan and cook until all the liquid as been absorbed.

SAVOURY PASTRY
(Basic 21)

250g	Flour
125g	Butter (diced)
50 ml	Mineral water
	Pinch of Salt

1. Sieve the flour, add the salt.
2. Rub in the butter using finger tips.
3. Add water and gently mix together.

SWEET PASTRY
(Basic 22)

250g	Flour
50g	Sugar
125g	Butter (diced)
	Pinch salt
1	Egg
	Vanilla essence (optional)
	Mineral water

1   Sieve the flour, add the salt and sugar.
2   Gently rub the butter to a sandy texture.
3   Add the beaten egg, allow the mixture to come together without force.
4   Cling film and refrigerate until needed.

PASTRY CREAM
(Basic 23)

2	Eggs
4	Egg yolks
75g	Caster sugar
400 ml	Milk
100 ml	Double cream
25g	Flour
½	Vanilla pod
1 tsp	Gelatine (optional)

1 Whisk the eggs, egg yolks and caster sugar together add the flour and whisk until smooth.
2 Place the milk, cream and vanilla in a saucepan and bring to the boil.
3 Whisk in half the milk to the egg mix, then return this mix back to the saucepan and return to the stove. Stir the sauce until it thickens.
4 If using leaf gelatine dissolve in the sauce while still on the heat. If using powdered gelatine, add gelatine to a little cold water and heat on the stove until all dissolved, then add to the pastry cream
5 Remove from the heat and dust the top with icing sugar (this stop a skin forming).

TRIFLE SPONGE
(Basic 24)

4	Eggs (slightly warm)
100g	Golden caster sugar
100g	plain flour (sieved)

1. Whisk the eggs then sprinkle on the sugar whilst still whisking.
2. Once at the sabayon stage gently fold in the flour.
3. Place on a lined Swiss roll tray.
4. Bake at 200C for 10-12 minutes.
5. Once out of the oven peel off the grease proof.
6. If using the sponge for a trifle, spread with jam and roll to resemble a Swiss roll.

STOCK SYRUP
(Basic 25)

75g	Sugar
100g	Water

1. Put both ingredients into a saucepan and bring to the boil
2. Simmer for 1 minute and remove from heat.

FRESH FRUIT SAUCE
(Basic 26)

200g	Raspberry / Strawberry
½	Lemon
	Stock Syrup (BASIC 25)

1   Blend the fruit and lemon juice, then pass through a sieve.
2   Add the stock syrup until you reach the correct consistency.
3   Add any flavourings if desired.

BUTTERSCOTCH SAUCE
(Basic 27)

100g	Soft Brown sugar
50g	Butter
25 ml	Double Cream

1   Place butter and sugar into a saucepan and bring to the boil, take off the heat and add the cream and mix in until smooth

CUSTARD
(Basic 28)

400 ml	Milk
100 ml	Double cream
100g	Sugar
5	Egg yolks
½	Vanilla pod

1   Put the milk and double cream and the split vanilla pod in a saucepan and bring to the boil

2   Whisk the sugar and egg yolks in a bowl until pale.

3   Add half of the boiling milk to the egg and sugar mix and mix well, return the mixture back to the remaining milk in the saucepan on a low heat and stir until the mixture coats the back of the spoon.

4   Pass custard through a strainer and cool over a bath of ice.

Note: You can add various flavourings to this sauce

YOGHURT SAUCE
(Basic 29)

300 ml	Natural yoghurt
½ small	Onion
1 tsp	Chives (chopped)
50g	Cucumber (peeled)
Pinch	Salt

1   Beat the yoghurt smooth and add the rest of the ingredients.

PEELED TOMATOES
(Basic 31)

1   Tomato

1   Score the top of the tomato.
2   Boil a small pan of water, once boiling remove from the heat.
3   Place in the tomato and wait until the skin starts to blister or become loose.
4   Remove tomato and peel off the skin.
5   Cut the tomato in half and remove the seeds.
6   You can now cut the tomato to the desired shape.

MEASUREMENT TABLE

(These weights are approximate equivalents)

Imperial Weights	Metric Weights	Imperial Weights	Metric Weights
¼ oz	5g	8 oz	200g
½ oz	10g	9 oz	225g
1 oz	25g	10 oz	250g
2 oz	50g	11 oz	275g
2 ½ oz	60g	12 oz	300g
3 oz	75g	13 oz	325g
4 oz	100g	14 oz	350g
5 oz	125g	15 oz	375g
6 oz	150g	16 oz	400g
7 oz	175g		

Imperial Weights	Metric Weights	Imperial Weights	Metric Weights
1 fl oz	25 ml	10 fl oz	250 ml
2 fl oz	50 ml	11 fl oz	275 ml
3 fl oz	75 ml	12 fl oz	300 ml
4 fl oz	100 ml	13 fl oz	325 ml
5 fl oz	125 ml	14 fl oz	350 ml
6 fl oz	150 ml	15 fl oz	375 ml
7 fl oz	175 ml	16 fl oz	400 ml
8 fl oz	200 ml	20 fl oz	500 ml
9 fl oz	225 ml	2 pt	1000 ml

4 oz = ¼ lb	5 fl oz = ¼ pt	250 ml = ¼ litre
8 oz = ½ lb	10 fl oz = ½ pt	500 ml = ½ litre
16 oz = 1 lb	15 fl oz = ¾ pt	1000 ml = 1 litre
	20 fl oz = 1 pt	
	2 pt = 1 qt	

Imperial	Metric	Imperial	Metric
¼ inch	½ cm	4 inch	10 cm
½ inch	1 cm	5 inch	12 cm
1 inch	2 cm	6 inch	15 cm
1 ½ inch	4 cm	7 inch	18 cm
2 inch	5 cm	10 inch	24cm
2 ½ inch	6 cm	12 inch	30 cm
3 inch	8 cm	18 inch	45 cm

OVEN TEMPERATURES

COOL	100	¼	225
	130	½	250
	140	1	275
	150	2	300
	160	3	325
MODERATE	180	4	350
	190	5	375
	200	6	400
HOT	220	7	425
	230	8	450
VERY HOT	250	9	500

Notes

Notes

<u>Notes</u>

INDEX

D

DOUBLE BUTTERFISH with citrus butter sauce	70

E

ESCOVEICITCH FISH	46

F

FILLET OF BEEF with a spiced sauce	92
FILLET OF LAMB with coconut sauce	87
FISH TEA	52
FISH SAUCE	156
FISH STOCK	155
FRESH FRUIT SAUCE	174

G

GLAZED DUCK with rum & honey sauce	90
GREEN BANANA CHIPS	122
GUINEA FOWL	100

J

JAMAICAN GINGER PUDDING	141
JAMACIAN ORANGE CREAMED ICE	150
JAMAICAN TILAPIA SALAD with green banana chips	44
JERK CHICKEN STUFFED with callaloo & bbq sauce	95
JERK CHICKEN TERRINE	48
JERK LOBSTER BAKED	63
JERK PORK FILLET	94
JERK SALMON	74
JERK SEASONING	168
JUNJA SAUCE	166

L

LAMB STOCK & SAUCE	157
LAYERED PARROT FISH	76
LAYERED VEGETABLES	111
LOBSTER AND SALTFISH CAKE	40

M

MANGO & PAWPAW TOWER	144
MANGO MAYONAISE	163
MIXED TROPICAL FRUIT TART	146
MIXED VEGETABLE GRATIN	123

O

OCHO RIOS CABBAGE	120
OKRA PARCELS with sweet pepper sauce	106
ONION SAUCE	165

ORANGE SAUCE 175

P
PAN ROAST TILAPIA served with tomato sauce . . . 68
PASTRY CREAM 172
PEELED TOMATOES 176
PINEAPPLE & BANANA CRUMBLE 132
PINEAPPLE TART 138
PUMPKIN PIE 140
PUMPKIN SOUP 32

R
RED PEPPER SAUCE 164
RICE & PEAS 170
ROAST DOCTOR FISH 78
ROAST VEGETABLES 126
RUNDOWN MACKERAL TART 80
RUM & RAISIN CHEESECAKE 129
RUM TRIFLE 130

S
SAVOURY PASTRY 171
SEAFOOD & CALLALOO TART 69
SPICED LAMB 89
SPICY CRAB AND VEGETABLE ROLLS . . . 56
SPICY TOMATO SAUCE 161
SPICY RED SNAPPER 72
STEAMED FISH with ginger butter sauce . . . 73
STEAMED BANANA PUDDING 136
STOCK SYRUP 173
SWEET PASTRY 171
SWEET POTATOES & ONION 122

T
THYME SAUCE 167
TONGA AND ROAST PEPPER SALAD . . . 39
TRIFLE SPONGE 173
TRIPLE CHOCOLATE DELIGHT 148
TUNA JERK STYLE 65

V
VEGETABLE RICE 110
VEGETABLE STOCK 158
VEGETARIAN CRUMBLE 112

Many cities now have a number of West Indian shops, all of which will have a good selection of ingredients from this book.

Acknowledgements

I would like to send many thanks to Duncan, for over 30 years of loyal support, the father I never had. Also thank you to my aunt Jean, uncle Peter and uncle George.

Thanks to Jim, Roz and Graham.

Thank you also to Joan, Nikki, Jo and Zubia, especially Joan for steeping in at 11th hour.

A big thank you to Tracey and my children, also my sister Marcia for putting up with me over the last few weeks. It took awhile but we got there in the end.

Last of all, thank you to my late mother and grandfather, for teaching me all they knew and instilling me with the secretes of life.